Our Faith and Worship

A Textbook of Islamic 'Aqa'id and ' Arkan

Upper elementary Level

Volume 2

Dr. Abidullah Ghazi
Dr. Tasneema Khatoon Ghazi

IQRA'
INTERNATIONAL EDUCATIONAL FOUNDATION
CHICAGO

Part of a Comprehensive and Systematic Program of Islamic Studies

A Textbook for the Program of 'Aqīdah and Fiqh Elementary Level

Our Faith and Worship Vol.2

Chief Program Editors
Dr. Abidullah al-Ansari Ghazi
(Ph.D., Study of Religion
Harvard University)

Tasneema Ghazi
(Ph.D., Curriculum-Reading
University of Minnesota)

Language Editing
Samina Mustapha

Reviewed by
Fadel Abdullah
(M.A. Arabic Islamic Studies,
University of Minnesota)

Dr. Khwaja Moinul Hassan
(Ph. D. English, Purdue University)

Typesetting
Sabeehuddin Khaja

Design
Laura Boyce
(B.F.A. Graphic Design,
University of Illinois at Chicago)

Printed February, 2010
Printed in U.S.A

Library of Congress Control Number 94-65696
ISBN # 1-56316-1-56316-060-9

Dedication

Prominent Imams of the Fiqh

Founders of the Major Schools of Islamic Shari'ah Who Studied the Qur'an and the Sunnah and Developed Principles of Fiqh And Organized the Knowledge of Islamic Shari'ah.

Imam Ja'far As-Sadiq (80-148 A.H./699-765 C.E.)

Imam Abu Hanifah an-Nu'man ibn Thabit (80-150 A.H./700-768 C.E.)

Imam Zaid ibn 'Ali (80-122 A.H./699-740 C.E.)

Imam Malik ibn 'Anas (93-179 A.H./711-796 C.E.)

Imam Muhammad ibn Idris Ash-Shafi'i (150-205 A.H./767-820 C.E.)

Imam Abu 'Abdullah Ahmad ibn Hanbal (164-241 A.H./780-855 C.E.)

May Allah سبحانه وتعالى Shower Them All with His Mercy

Quoted in Iyad Hilal, Studies in Usul Al-Fiqh, pp 97-123
Islamic Cultural Workshop, Walnut, CA

Table of Contents

OUR FAITH AND WORSHIP, Volume 2

IQRA's Note: For Teachers and Parents

The textbook *Our Faith and Worship, Volume 2*, is written for the Elementary Level as a part of IQRA's Comprehensive and Systematic program of *'Aqīdah* and *Fiqh*. Volume 1 covered several important questions concerning *'Aqīdah* and *Salāh* (Prayer) appropriate for ages 8-10. This volume concerns itself with *Ṣawm*, *Zakāh* and *Ḥajj*. The teacher may not find the answers to all of the student's questions in this volume, however, the Junior Level textbook, *Islamic 'Aqīdah and Fiqh*, and Senior level textbook deals with the same subject in greater depth and detail.

The program of *'Aqīdah* and *Fiqh* is presented at four levels: Kindergarten, elementary, junior and senior. The textbooks are prepared by well-known scholars for appropriate levels.

This textbook covers the *Siyam*, *Ḥajj*, *Zakāh*, *Jihād*, Sources of Islamic *Sharī'ah* and *Ḥalāl* and *Ḥarām*. The last three topics are introduced at the elementary level for the first time and we hope these will greatly enhance young students' understanding of these important areas of *Fiqh*. An Appendix on *Asmā Allah al-Ḥusnā* may be used to memorize these Beautiful Names or read them as an additional lesson.

Workbooks for these texts are also being prepared by educators to provide the students with important exercises and to aid in the development of problem solving, sequencing, drawing inferences, evaluating, analyzing and synthesizing skills. The workbooks are an essential part of IQRA's educational efforts and must be used for best results of educating and developing creative thinking.

This limited edition is being published for general review, opinions and field-testing. We request all teachers and parents to inform us of their opinions and suggestions. We shall gratefully accept positive suggestions to improve the text and enhance its usefulness.

IQRA's efforts toward producing quality Islamic educational material written by scholars has won worldwide appreciation and *Al-Ḥamdu li-Allāh*, IQRA's publications are currently in use at many Islamic schools throughout North America and are gaining acceptance all over the world.

We are grateful to Allah ﷻ for this unique success and appeal to all concerned Muslims to make a special *Du'ā'* for us and to participate in this Islamic endeavor by becoming:

1. Ansar of IQRA' educational program
2. Members of the IQRA' Book Club

It is through our joint endeavors that we can build IQRA' Foundation as a viable and professional Islamic educational institution. May Allāh ﷻ help us to fulfill His mission.

Chief editors

Jum'ah, Dhu al-Ḥijjah 15th, 1416
Friday, May 3rd, 1996

Lesson 1

THE ṢIYĀM: FASTING

The *Ṣiyām* or *Ṣawm*, the fasting in the month of *Ramaḍan*, is a *Rukn* (Pillar) of Islam. Fasting during *Ramaḍan* is a Fard, an obligation, for every adult Muslim.

Allah ﷻ says in the Qur'an:

يَٰٓأَيُّهَا ٱلَّذِينَ ءَامَنُوا۟ كُتِبَ
عَلَيْكُمُ ٱلصِّيَامُ كَمَا كُتِبَ عَلَى ٱلَّذِينَ مِن قَبْلِكُمْ
لَعَلَّكُمْ تَتَّقُونَ ١٨٣

"O you who Believe! The fasting is prescribed to you as it was prescribed to those before you in order for you to become *Muttaqī* (righteous).
(*Al-Baqarah* 2:179)

Allah ﷻ has prescribed fasting for all peoples in the past. The followers of many earlier religions observed fasting. The purpose of fasting in Islam is to make us Muttaqun (righteous).

Muttaqī is an Arabic word which has no precise English translation. A *Muttaqī* is one who has *Taqwā*, the fear and love of Allah ﷻ. A *Muttaqī* is a Righteous person, who follows what is *Ḥalāl* and avoids what is *Ḥarām*. A *Muttaqī* is one who always follows the Right Path of Islam and leads his or her life according to Islamic *Sharī'ah*.

The purpose of fasting then is to create *Taqwā* in our hearts and to make us *Muttaqīn*. The Fasting, if observed properly, prepares us to follow the right path of Islam and avoid the wrong path of disbelief.

Siyam means "to refrain from" or "not to do something." Allah ﷻ has asked us to stay away during the month of Ramadan from eating and drinking from dawn to sunset.

We must fast every day in the month of *Ramaḍān* from *aṣ-Subh aṣ-Sādiq*, (pre-dawn), to the Maghrib (the sunset). The month of *Ramaḍān* is the ninth month of the Islamic *Hijrah* calendar.

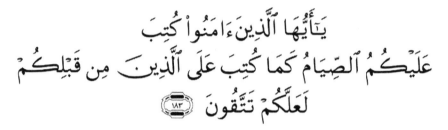

The Islamic era started with the *Hijrah* (migration) of Rasūl-Allāh ﷺ from Makkah to Madinah. The Islamic calendar follows the lunar system. Islamic months start with the sighting of the new moon and end with the sighting of the new moon. Each month has twenty-nine or thirty days, depending on when the moon is sighted.

A true *Ṣiyām* is not merely to give up food and drink but it is also to give up bad habits. When fasting we should not lie, fight, get angry or use bad language. Fasting teaches us to control ourselves. Rasūl-Allāh ﷺ said:

"If someone does not give up falsehood in his words and actions, Allah has no need for his giving up food and drink."
(*Al-Bukhārī*)

If we learn to control both our hunger and our bad temper in *Ramaḍān*, Allah ﷻ will help us to give up bad habits forever. The true reward of the *Ṣiyām* is to gain the pleasure of Allah ﷻ.

Prophet Muḥammad ﷺ told us that Allah ﷻ says:

"Every action of a human being is for himself, except the Fasting, The Fasting is solely for my pleasure and I shall Myself give reward for it."
(*Al-Bukhārī*)

Fasting teaches us to do what Allah ﷻ wants us to do. For Muslims, *Ramaḍān* is a great opportunity to show our readiness to submit to the commands of Allah ﷻ and make His Will foremost in our lives. At the same time, going without food and drink allows us to acknowledge their importance in our lives, and to see what a debt of gratitude we owe to Allah ﷻ for being the Provider. All of this serves to make us more conscious of Allah's love for us; thus it makes us more eager to want to please Him continuously. This is the meaning of *Taqwā*.

WE HAVE LEARNED:

- The *Ṣiyām* is a *Rukn*, Pillar of Islam.
- Fasting means giving up food, drinks, and bad habits.
- The Fasting allows us to gain *Taqwā* (righteousness) and become Muttaqi (Righteous).

DO WE KNOW THESE WORDS?

Hijrah, *Muttaqī*, precise, prescribed, *Sharī'ah*, *Ṣawm*, *Ṣiyām*, *aṣ-Subh aṣ-Ṣādiq*, *Taqwā*

Lesson 2

THE MONTH OF THE QUR'ĀN

Ramaḍān is a special month of Allah's Favors, Mercy and Blessings. Allah ﷻ calls *Ramaḍān* His own month. Although the whole month of *Ramaḍān* is full of blessings, it gives us three very special blessings. First, it is the month of *Ṣiyām,* which has its true reward from Allah ﷻ. Second, it is the month of the Revelation of the Qur'ān which is true guidance and mercy for all humanity. And finally, in this month comes the *Lailat al-Qadr* (read as Lailatu-(a)l-Qadr) which is better than one thousand months.

Ramaḍān is the month of the Qur'ān. It was revealed in this month. Allah ﷻ says in the Qur'ān:

شَهْرُ رَمَضَانَ ٱلَّذِىٓ أُنزِلَ فِيهِ ٱلْقُرْءَانُ هُدًى لِّلنَّاسِ
وَبَيِّنَـٰتٍ مِّنَ ٱلْهُدَىٰ وَٱلْفُرْقَانِ ۚ

"The month of *Ramaḍān* , during which the Qur'ān was revealed, a guidance for humankind, and a clear proof of the guidance and criterion of right and wrong.
(*Al-Baqarah 2:185*)

The Qur'an was revealed in the night of *Lailat al-Qadr*, the "Night of Power."

Allah ﷻ says in the Qur'ān:

إِنَّآ أَنزَلْنَـٰهُ فِى لَيْلَةِ ٱلْقَدْرِ ﴿١﴾ وَمَآ أَدْرَىٰكَ مَا لَيْلَةُ ٱلْقَدْرِ ﴿٢﴾
لَيْلَةُ ٱلْقَدْرِ خَيْرٌ مِّنْ أَلْفِ شَهْرٍ ﴿٣﴾

"We have revealed this (Qur'ān) in the Night of Power (*Lailat al-Qadr*). And what do you know what the Night of Power is? The Night of Power is better than a thousand months."
(*Al-Qadr 97:1-3*)

Rasul-Allāh ﷺ did not tell us exactly when *Lailat al-Qadr*, the Night of Power, occurs. He advised us to seek this Blessed Night in the last odd nights of the *Ramaḍān* . Many people believe it to be the night of the twenty-seventh of *Ramaḍān* . Most Muslims try to seek it in the last ten nights by offering special prayers, readings of the Qur'ān and

being most charitable to others.
Rasul-Allāh ﷺ said about blessings of *Ramaḍān*:

"It is a month whose beginning is Mercy, whose middle is forgiveness and whose end is freedom from the Fire."
(*Ibn Khuzaimah*)

In *Ramaḍān* we offer the special *Ṣalāh* of *Tarāwiḥ*. The *Tarāwīḥ* is a *Sunnah* and is offered with the *'Isha'* prayer. Every community makes special preparations for the *Tarāwiḥ* in the Masajid. The *Tarāwiḥ* prayers are generally offered behind an *'Imām*, who is a *Ḥāfiẓ* and *Qāri'* of the Qur'ān. A *Ḥāfiẓ* is one who has memorized the entire Qur'ān. A *Qāri'* is one who has learned the rules of Qur'anic recitation and is able to recite beautifully.

During *Ramaḍān Tarāwīḥ*, a *Ḥāfiẓ* reads portions of the Qur'ān. He completes the Qur'ān sometime during the last ten days of *Ramaḍān*. If there is no *Ḥāfiẓ* available we should read as much Qur'ān as possible in the *Tarāwīḥ*. The *Tarāwīḥ* can also be offered individually.

For the Believers, *Ramaḍān* is a month of great happiness and celebration. We should try to complete the reading of the Qur'ān, with meaning, at least one time during the month of *Ramaḍān*. Rasūl-Allāh ﷺ completed the reading of the Qur'ān with the Angel Jibrīl ؑ each *Ramaḍān*. In his last *Ramaḍān* he completed the Qur'ān with Angel Jibrīl ؑ twice.

Ramaḍān is a special month of charity. Rasūl-Allah ﷺ was the most charitable person who ever lived. In the month of *Ramaḍān* his charity increased many times more. We must be especially hospitable and charitable in the month of *Ramaḍān*. We should invite people to *Iftar* (breaking the fast) with us. We can also take our food to our Islamic Center or *Masjid* and share it with others. We must show special kindnesses to those Muslims who are in need and require our support.

Every charity performed in *Ramaḍān* receives special reward from Allah ﷻ.
Rasūl-Allāh ﷺ said:

"When a Muslim performs Fard 'Ibadat during Ramadan he receives seventy times more reward (than what he normally would receive)."
(*Mishkat al-Masabih*)

WE HAVE LEARNED:

- *Ramaḍān* is the month in which the Qur'ān was revealed.
- It is a month of Lailat al-Qadr.
- It is a month of special charity and hospitality.

DO WE KNOW THESE WORDS?

Ibadat, Ḥāfiẓ, Lailat al-Qari, Qari, Tarāwiḥ

Lesson 3

THE FASTING: AN OBLIGATION

There are two kinds of fasting, *Farḍ* (obligatory), and *Nafl* (optional). The *Fard* fast is performed in the month of *Ramaḍān* each year. If one misses the fast of *Ramaḍān* for some genuine reason, he or she should make up for it. The Nafl fast could be performed any time except the two days of Id, the Id al-Fitr and Id al-Adha.

These are some Adab (rules) and obligations of the Siyam that we must follow.

The Suḥūr: It is *Sunnah* to get up for *Suḥūr* and eat something. The time of *Suḥūr* is anytime after midnight and before *aṣ-Ṣubh aṣ-Ṣādiq* (pre-dawn).

The Niyyah:
Niyyah (intention), of the Fast. The *Niyyah* of the fasting is:

بِصَوْمِ غَدٍ نَوَيْتُ مِنْ شَهْرِ رَمَضَانَ

I intend to fast tomorrow, for the month of *Ramaḍān.*

One can make the intention in one's heart or say it aloud in Arabic or in any other language.

Stop Eating: One must stop eating at *aṣ-Ṣubh aṣ-Ṣādiq* (pre-dawn). The time of pre-dawn is just before the break of dawn. It is shortly prior to the time of the beginning of the *Fajr Ṣalāh.*

Invalidation of the Fast: Allah ﷻ requires us to abstain from food, drink and smoking. If we do any of these by mistake, our fast breaks and requires the *Qaḍā*. *Qaḍā'* means to make up for the missed fast at a time after *Ramaḍān* is over. If a women starts her menstruation then her fast breaks. However, if one forgets and eats or drinks accidentally (or does any of the things that break the fast by mistake), the fast remains unbroken. For breaking the fast intentionally, without a valid reason, the Qada is *Kaffarah.* The *Kaffarah* of a fast is to feed sixty hungry people or to fast continuously for two months.

'Ifṭār: Soon after the sunset, one must have *'Ifṭār* (opening the fast) with this Du'ā':

اللَّهُمَّ لَكَ صُمْتُ ، وَبِكَ آمَنْتُ ،
وَعَلَيْكَ تَوَكَّلْتُ ، وَعَلَى رِزْقِكَ أَفْطَرْتُ

O Allah I have fasted for Your sake, and I believe in You, and on you I rely and with your food I break my *Ṣiyām*.

It is a *Sunnah* to open the fast with dates and water. It is better to have a light *'Ifṭār*, offer the *Ṣalah* of *Maghrib* and then have the dinner.

The *Ṣalāh* of *Tarāwīḥ*: It is a *Sunnah* to offer *Tarāwīḥ* in the nights of *Ramaḍān* . The *Tarāwīḥ* is offered after the *Ṣalāh* of *'Ishā'*. There is greater reward for offering the *Tarāwīḥ* with *Jamā'ah* at the *Masjid*.

Ḥarām Fasting: Fasting is an act of *'Ibādah*. An act of *'Ibādah* is to do things as required by Allah ﷻ and to avoid those things that are forbidden by Him. It is also an act of *'Ibādah* not to fast on certain days. There are five days on which the fasting is *Ḥarām*: *'Īd al-Fiṭr*, *'Id al-'Aḍḥā* and *'Ayyām at-Tashrīq* (the days of *Ḥajj*: 11th 12th and 13th of *Dhū al-Ḥijjah*).

Sunnah, and *Nafl* Fasting: There are many other Fasts that are *Sunnah* or *Nafl*. There is a special reward for those fasts and there is no punishment for not fasting on those days.

'Īd al-Fiṭr: *'Id al-Fiṭr* means "the feast of opening of the Fast". *Ramaḍān* comes to an end with the sighting of the moon of *Shawwāl*, the month which follows *Ramaḍān* in the Muslim calendar. After the sighting of the moon there is no *Tarāwīḥ* and no fasting.

It is a *Sunnah* to break the fast on *'Īd* day by eating a date or something after the *Fajr*. On the first of *Shawwāl* all Muslims celebrate *'Id al-Fiṭr*.

The *Sadaqah al-Fiṭr* must be offered before the *'Īd* prayer. It can be offered as money or the equivalent of 4-5 dollars.

WE HAVE LEARNED:

- There are two kinds of fasting, *fard* and *nafl*.
- In the *Ṣiyām* we abstain from food, drink and smoking.
- We start the fast at *aṣ-Ṣubh aṣ-Ṣādiq* (pre-dawn) and break it soon after the sunset.
- *Ramaḍān* is the month of the Qur'ān.

DO WE KNOW THESE WORDS?

Abstain, *'Ayyam at-Tashrīq*, *Fard*, genuine, *'Īd al-Fiṭr*, invalidation, menstruation, *Nafl*, *Wājib*.

Lesson 4

THE ZAKĀH

To give the *Zakah* is a *Rukn*, a Pillar of Islam. Like the Salah and Sawm and Hajj, it is an Islamic *Fard* (obligation). In the Qur'ān it is always mentioned alongside the *Ṣalāh*. The *Zakāh* (or Zakat) is an Arabic word which means to make something purified. It also means to make something grow.

There is no English word which can correctly describe its meanings. It is sometimes translated as Poor Due, Charity or Tithe. None of these words explain its true meaning and spirit. By giving the *Zakāh* we purify our wealth. Allah ﷻ blesses our wealth and often causes it to increase.

The *Zakāh* means to share the wealth given to us by Allah ﷻ with the poor and the needy. The *Zakāh* is the right of needy Muslims to share in the wealth of those Muslims whom Allah ﷻ has blessed with more than what meets their needs.

The Qur'ān says:

وَٱلَّذِينَ فِىٓ أَمْوَٰلِهِمْ حَقٌّ مَّعْلُومٌ ﴿٢٤﴾ لِّلسَّآئِلِ وَٱلْمَحْرُومِ ﴿٢٥﴾

And in their (Muslims') wealth there is a recognized right
for the needy and the poor."
(*Al-Ma'ārij 70:24-25*)

By giving the *Zakāh,* we clean our wealth and make it pure. There is great *Barakah* in giving. Allah ﷻ blesses our wealth, purifies it and makes it grow. The Qur'ān commands Rasūl-Allāh ﷺ:

خُذْ مِنْ أَمْوَٰلِهِمْ صَدَقَةً تُطَهِّرُهُمْ وَتُزَكِّيهِم بِهَا وَصَلِّ عَلَيْهِمْ ۖ

"Take from their wealth charity (*Zakāh*), to purify them and make
them grow and pray for them...."
(*At-Tawbah 9:103*)

Just as we need to take showers to clean our bodies and we wash our clothes to remove the dirt, so we must give the *Zakāh* to make our earnings clean of any impurity. And just as we feel fresh after a bath and feel better with clean clothes, so does a Believer feel after giving the *Zakāh*.

As Muslims we know everything we have is a gift from Allah ﷻ. Allah ﷻ has given us many things free without any effort on our part. For other things we have to work to earn them. But even the ability to work and earn are precious gifts from Allah ﷻ. There are many people who can not work and earn money. They are always dependent upon others to survive. We have special responsibility to care for them.

We must remember that giving the *Zakāh* is an Islamic duty, an act of *'Ibādah*. The purpose of giving the *Zakāh* is not to earn favors from those who receive it. The only favor a Believer seeks in helping others is the pleasure of Allah ﷻ.

The purpose of all *'Ibādāt* in Islam is to allow the Muslim to be worthy of Allah's ﷻ favor, and therefore to move closer to Him. A Believer must perform all *'Ibādāt* with sincerity. We should seek the reward of our *'Ibādāt* from Allah ﷻ alone.

Islam teaches us that we Muslims are one *'Ummah*, one family in Islam. As in any family, the members have responsibilities toward one another; each member of the Muslim Ummah has a duty to care for the others.

Rasūl-Allāh ﷺ said:

"You will see the Muslims in their mercy, love and concern for each other as one body: when one part of it is hurt the whole body feels its pain and restlessness"
(*Al-Bukhārī, Muslim*)

The *Zakāh* is a practical way to show our love and concern for our Muslim family. Sharing our wealth with other Muslims shows our concern for them. By sharing and caring we come closer to our Muslim brothers and sisters, while creating a more economically-balanced *'Ummah*.

WE HAVE LEARNED:

- The *Zakāh* is a *Rukn* (Pillar), of Islam.
- Giving the *Zakāh* purifies our wealth and makes it grow.
- By sharing the blessings of Allah ﷻ with others we show them our love and concern.

DO YOU KNOW THESE WORDS?

Balanced, *'Ibādāt*, purify, share, *'Ummah*, *Zakāh*

Lesson 5

THE NIṢĀB FOR THE ZAKĀH

The zakah is a Fard, an obligation, on every Muslim who has a Nisab. The Zakah, however, is the minimum that a Muslim is required to pay to help other human beings. Islam teaches us to be generous and kind to others. Islam has established special rights for parents, relatives, neighbors and the needy. There is no limit to our kindness, generosity or charity. We should give as much as we can to help others and to support any good cause.

Islam teaches us to give the *Ṣadaqah* (charity) and *Zakāh* to those who need our help. Islam also encourages us to give *Hadāyā* (gifts) to our family and friends to show them our love and concern.

When we do any good work we must have pure intentions. A pure intention means that our aim in doing good things is to please Allah ﷻ alone. It means we should not ask for any favors in return for our goodness.

The giving of *Ṣadaqah* is like doing a business with Allah ﷻ. When we help others by giving money, we are in essence giving a goodly loan (*Qard Hasanah*) to Allah ﷻ. Allah ﷻ returns the loan by rewarding us with *barakah* (blessings), often in ways we may not realize. The *Zakāh* is also a form of *Ṣadaqah*, but it is *Farḍ*, whereas *Ṣadaqah* is optional.

To pay the *Zakāh* is an obligation for every adult Muslim, if he or she has a *Niṣāb*. The *Niṣāb* is the minimun amount of wealth that one must possess before one is obligated to pay the *Zakāh*.

The following are some of the items for which we must pay the *Zakāh*:

1. Money, silver and gold
2. Land and Property
3. Animals
4. Grains, vegetables and fruit crops

We should pay the *Zakāh* if we have any amount of wealth which equals the *Niṣāb* or is more than it. The *Niṣāb* of each item of value differs. The calculation of *Zakāh* on different types of wealth is a highly sophisticated science whose details are seen in *Fiqh* books or found through the *Faqih* (Fiqh Scholar).

However, the *Zakāh* for money is 2.5% of one's savings for the year. The *Zakāh* becomes *Farḍ* for a person who possesses wealth according to *Niṣāb* or in excess of it for one complete year.

If a Muslim is in debt, he should first pay off the debt before he pays the *Zakāh*. The payment of one's debt is a very important religious duty of a believer. If a Muslim's debts are in excess of the *Niṣāb* of the *Zakāh*, he must not pay the *Zakāh* but pay off his debts. If his debts are less than the amount of the *Niṣāb* he must pay *Zakāh* on the remaining amount.

One year must pass on the wealth before the *Zakāh* becomes obligatory. If one whole year has not passed and one spends, transfers or loses wealth, it is not necessary to pay the *Zakāh*. Everyone who has a *Niṣab* must calculate it each year to pay the *Zakāh*.

Many people prefer to pay the *Zakāh* in the blessed month of *Ramaḍān* , although it is not necessary to pay it in any certain month. Charity given in *Ramaḍān* brings greater *Barakah* than usual.

WE HAVE LEARNED:

- Islam encourages charity and generosity.
- The *Zakāh* is a *Farḍ* for every Muslim who has wealth according to *Niṣāb*.
- There is a different *Niṣāb* for different items of value.

DO YOU KNOW THESE WORDS?

Niṣāb, *Qard Hasanah*, recommended, required, *Ṣadaqah*.

Lesson 6

THE PAYMENT OF ZAKĀH

The obligation to pay the *Zakāh* is a special favor of Allah ﷻ to Muslims. Only a Muslim is required to pay the *Zakāh*. Non-Muslims are not obligated to pay the *Zakāh*. In Islamic Societies in the past only the Muslims were required to pay the *Zakāh* to the government. The non-Muslims paid other kind of taxes.

If a non-Muslim accepts Islam the *Zakāh* becomes obligatory upon him. However, he does not pay the *Zakāh* for his previous years as a non-Muslim.

An insane Muslim or a young child (minor), even though he may possess *Niṣāb*, is not required to pay the *Zakāh*.

Allah ﷻ has described in the Qur'ān eight categories of the people who can receive the *Zakāh*:

إِنَّمَا ٱلصَّدَقَٰتُ لِلۡفُقَرَآءِ وَٱلۡمَسَٰكِينِ وَٱلۡعَٰمِلِينَ عَلَيۡهَا وَٱلۡمُؤَلَّفَةِ
قُلُوبُهُمۡ وَفِي ٱلرِّقَابِ وَٱلۡغَٰرِمِينَ وَفِي سَبِيلِ ٱللَّهِ وَٱبۡنِ ٱلسَّبِيلِۖ
فَرِيضَةٗ مِّنَ ٱللَّهِۗ وَٱللَّهُ عَلِيمٌ حَكِيمٞ ٦٠

"*Sadaqat* (*Zakāh*) is for the poor, and for the needy, and for those who work to collect the funds, and for those whose hearts are to be won over, and for the ransoming of the slaves, and for those in debt, and for the cause of Allah, and for the hospitality of the wayfarers. This is an obligation (*Farḍ*) from Allah, and Allah is All-Knowing and All-Wise.
(*At-Tawbah 9:60*)

The *Zakāh* could be spent on the poor or those who do not have enough money to survive.

The *Zakāh* could be given to the needy person who depends upon others for support. The needy may include the handicapped, or the orphans, or the widows, or those who are in temporary need.

Officials who work to collect the *Zakāh* can get their salary from the *Zakāh*. The *Zakāh* collectors were appointed by the Islamic state to collect the *Zakāh*.

The *Zakāh* could also be given to those whose hearts are to be won. These are new converts who are struggling to establish themselves in the Muslim community and need help. These could also be non-Muslims who need help and their friendship could be won for the Muslim community. They may also be attracted to Islam due to the generosity of Muslim society. (Non-Muslims could also be helped by Muslims through other forms of charity or gifts.) Rasūlullāh ﷺ and his *Sahabah* have set beautiful examples of helping every one in need, be they Muslims or non-Muslims.

In the past, slavery was common. Islam especially encouraged the freeing of slaves. It is a great act of charity to spend *Zakāh* money to free a slave from bondage. The *Zakāh* can be used for both freeing a slave or freeing an innocent person from jail. In many countries parents sell their children into slave labor due to poverty. We can use the *Zakāh* funds to help prevent all forms of slavery and bondage, including the bondage of ignorance.

The *Zakāh* money could be used to help those who are in debt. Many people who are in need go to others or to banks and borrow money on high interest. Due to their limited income they find it hard to pay off their debts. The *Zakāh* money could be used to help them.

An important purpose of the *Zakāh* is to pay those who work in the Way of Allah. Working in the Way of Allah means to support an Islamic cause. All those things which promote the cause of Islam could be supported from *Zakāh.*

The allowance for helping wayfarers had special significance in the past when travel was difficult and dangerous. Even today many travellers get stranded due to theft or personal losses. One could always help a traveller in need from the *Zakāh* funds.

The System of *Zakāh* is established by Allah ﷻ for the benefit of the *'Ummah.* The *Zakāh* is a serious obligation which every Muslim must fulfill.

WE HAVE LEARNED:

- Only those Muslims who have the *Niṣāb* are required to pay the *Zakāh.*
- The Qur'ān describes the catagories of those to whom the *Zakāh* must be paid.
- Rasūl-Allāh ﷺ has set beautiful examples of helping everyone, Muslims and non-Muslims alike.

DO WE KNOW THESE WORDS?

possession, property, recommended, required

Lesson 7

THOSE WHO CANNOT RECEIVE THE ZAKĀH

The *Zakāh* is the right of those who need the support of the community. Islam teaches us to take care of the family and close relatives. Because it is our obligation to care for our families continuously, we cannot deprive the poor and needy of *Zakāh* by giving or receiving it from family members. In other words, tending to the needs of family is a natural responsibility, and must be a constant priority. Giving *Zakāh* to our parents, for example, would be depriving those who really need it of their share of our wealth. Unfortunately, we often forget the less fortunate of our society.

For this reason, *Zakāh* exists to remind us people who have wealth according to *Niṣāb* must pay the *Zakāh* and not receive it. The *Zakāh* is the right of those who are below the *Niṣāb* level.

The *Zakāh* money is specifically for the Muslim community. The non-Muslims in an Islamic state could be helped by other sources of *Bait al-Māl*, the State Treasury. On an individual level we must help the needy non-Muslims through the *Ṣadaqah* and gifts. Only those non-Muslims can be helped whose favor might strengthen the Islamic community.

Anyone who is from the family of Rasūl-Allāh ﷺ (*Ahl al-Bait*) cannot receive the *Zakāh*. In several religions, the priestly class and decendents of the religious teachers became so important that everyone started helping them in order to gain favor or blessings. Rasūl-Allāh ﷺ forbade the payment of the *Zakāh* for his family fearing that they might receive all the money at the expense of the poor and needy.

Rasūl-Allāh's family, *'Ahl al-Bait* deserve special consideration from us. If they need our support we should help them through gifts. But in Islam there is no special merit in giving them money to gain *barakah* as opposed to giving to the needy and the poor.

We should follow Allah's Commands and give our *Zakāh* to those whom He ordains. And we should never take someone's right in receiving the *Zakāh* if we do not deserve it.

The *Zakāh* is only the minimum amount we are required to pay if we have *Niṣāb*. Allah ﷻ enjoins upon us charity. A *sadaqah* and no-interest loans are described by Allah ﷻ as Qard Hasanah (Beautiful loans) to Him. He promises great return for this loan:

مَّن ذَا ٱلَّذِى يُقْرِضُ ٱللَّهَ قَرْضًا حَسَنًا فَيُضَٰعِفَهُۥ لَهُۥٓ أَضْعَافًا كَثِيرَةً

"Who is it that will give to Allah a goodly loan, so that He may give it interest manifold..."
(*Al-Baqarah 2:245*)

For Muslims it is much better to help others with excess wealth and receive barakah from Allah ﷻ than to put our money in the bank to earn interest. As Muslims we must be generous and charitable to everyone, Muslim or non-Muslim. It is our duty to look after our fellow human beings, as well as all living things.

WE HAVE LEARNED:

- Every Muslim is responsible for his or her family. *Zakāh*, however, is not intended for one's immediate family but rather for the larger Muslim family.
- The *Zakāh* must be given to those who deserve it most.
- We must love *'Ahl al-Bait* of Rasūl-Allāh ﷺ and help them, if they need it, but not through *Zakāh*.

DO WE KNOW THESE WORDS?

'Ahl al-Bait, merit, *Niṣāb*, ordain, priestly

Lesson 8

ḤAJJ: THE PILGRIMAGE TO MAKKAH

The *Ḥajj* is the pilgrimage to *Bait Allah* (the House of Allah), in Makkah. The *Ḥajj* is a *Rukn* of Islam and it takes place in the month of *Dhū al-Ḥijjah*.

Bait Allah is the first house of worship built to honor Allah ﷻ alone. It was first built by Prophet Adam ﷺ. The children of Adam ﷺ worshipped Allah ﷻ in the *Ka'bah*. However, as time passed people forgot both about the teachings of Adam ﷺ and the the House of Allah ﷻ. Makkah became a barren and deserted land. Eventually, no one knew where the *Ka'bah* was.

Allah ﷻ commanded Prophet Ibrahim ﷺ to go to Makkah and build this House once again. He was asked to invite all human beings to come to Makkah and make the *Ḥajj* to that Holy Place. We shall briefly describe the story of Ibrahim ﷺ and his family and the building of *Bait Allah* in the next two lessons. You can also read this story in *The Stories of The Prophets of Allah, Volume II.*

Allah ﷻ says in the Qur'ān:

إِنَّ أَوَّلَ بَيْتٍ وُضِعَ لِلنَّاسِ لَلَّذِى
بِبَكَّةَ مُبَارَكًا وَهُدًى لِّلْعَٰلَمِينَ ﴿٩٦﴾

Indeed! It is the first House (of Allah) built for all human beings in the city of Makkah which is a blessed place of Guidance for all humankind.
(*Al 'Imran 3:96*)

Al-Masjid al-Harām, "the Sacred Mosque", is another name of *Bait Allah.* In the center of the *Masjid* is the *Ka'bah.* The *Ka'bah* is the most sacred building in the *Masjid al-Harām.* During the *Ḥajj* and the *'Umrah*, the pilgrims are required to make *Ṭawāf* (circling) around the *Ka'bah.* The best *Nafl 'Ibādah* in the *Ḥaram* is to perform the *Ṭawāf* around the *Ka'bah.* Circling the *Ka'bah* seven times counts as one *Ṭawāf.*

Sometime after the death of Prophet 'Ibrāhīm ﷺ and Prophet 'Ismā'īl ﷺ people forgot *Tawḥid* (worship of Allah alone). They also forgot the good teachings of their prophets. Like their idol-worshiping neighbors they invented and fashioned many idols, gods and goddesses. They started many evil practices.

Bait Allah became a House of Idols. Instead of worshiping the One True God, Allah, people started worshiping idols made of wood, metal, and stone.

Allah سبحانه وتعالى sent His final Prophet Muhammad, *Salla Allahu 'alai-hi wa Sallam*, to teach Islam, the religion of 'Ibrāhīm عليه السلام, to all humanity. Rasūl-Allāh ﷺ cleansed the *Ka'bah* by removing the idols.

But more important than cleaning the *Ka'bah* were his teachings which cleansed the hearts of the people from all kinds of *Shirk* and *Kufr*. *Shirk* means to accept other gods besides Allah. *Kufr* is to deny the existence of Allah and to be ungrateful for His Favors.

Rasūl-Allāh ﷺ once again established Allah's true religion, Islam, and taught how to worship Allah and lead a moral life. Before his death, he made a pilgrimage to Makkah with thousands of his *Ṣaḥābah* and showed them how to perform the *Ḥajj*. He told his *'Ummah*:

> "O people! *Ḥajj* has been made as a duty for you, so perform *Ḥajj*."
> (*Sahih Muslim*)

WE HAVE LEARNED:
- *Ḥajj* means the pilgrimage to *Bait Allah*, the House of Allah, in Makkah.
- *Bait Allah* was first built by Prophet Adam عليه السلام and then by Prophet 'Ibrāhīm عليه السلام and his son Prophet 'Ismā'īl عليه السلام.
- Rasūl-Allāh ﷺ showed us how to make the *Ḥajj*.

DO YOU KNOW THESE WORDS?
Bait Allah, barren, *Kufr*, *Masjid al-Ḥarām*, perform, Pilgrimage, *Shirk*, *Tawāf*, *Tawḥīd*, *'Umrah*

Lesson 9

THE STORY OF MAKKAH

Bait Allah, ("the House of Allah ﷻ"), or the *Ka'bah*, is located in the city of Makkah in Arabia. The founding of the City and the building of *Bait Allah* is a very beautiful story.

About four thousand years ago, in the city of Harrān, lived 'Āzar, the idol maker. An intelligent and beautiful boy was born to 'Āzar. He was named 'Ibrāhīm. 'Āzar wanted to train his boy in the art of idol making. However, Allah ﷻ chose 'Ibrāhīm to become His prophet and the father of many prophets.

Allah ﷻ gave 'Ibrāhīm ﷺ His guidance and blessed him with *Hikmah*, the Wisdom. As he grew, he opposed all forms of idol worship. Nimrūd, the powerful king of Harrān, had declared himself a god and ignorant people started worshiping him. 'Ibrāhīm told people, "Our Lord is Allah who has created every thing and to whom all that dies returns."

Nimrūd was so enraged with 'Ibrāhīm ﷺ that he made a large bonfire. He put 'Ibrāhīm ﷺ into that fire, but Allah ﷻ turned the fire into a garden and 'Ibrāhīm walked out of it safely and unhurt.

Allah ﷻ asked 'Ibrāhīm to take his wife Sarah and his family and followers and to settle in a land called Kan'ān. Later this land was called Palestine.

'Ibrāhīm lived to be old but he had no children. During his travels in Egypt, a country in North Africa, 'Ibrāhīm ﷺ took another wife Hājar. Hājar was a pious and faithful lady. Allah ﷻ blessed 'Ibrāhīm and Hājar with a son called 'Ismā'īl.

Now Sarah felt jealous to see 'Ibrāhīm's attention turn to his second wife and child. She wanted Hājar and the child to leave her household.

Allah ﷻ had better plans for Hājar and 'Ismā'īl. He asked 'Ibrāhīm ﷺ to take the mother and the child to the barren valley of *Bakkah* (later known as Makkah) and leave them there alone.

As 'Ibrāhīm left Hājar and only his child alone in the deserted valley of Bakkah, 'Ibrāhīm's heart was distressed but he was sure that Allah ﷻ had some plan, however hard it was for 'Ibrāhīm to understand.

Hājar asked him, ″Are you leaving us here because of Allah′s Commands or your own?″

″On Allah′s Command,″ replied 'Ibrāhīm.

″If it is a Command of Allah, then I accept His decision with pleasure,″ replied Hājar, accepting the descision of Allah.

'Ibrāhīm raised his hands and prayed to Allah:

″O My Lord, I have made some of my offspring to live in a valley without cultivation by your Sacred House: in order that they may establish regular prayer: So fill the hearts of some people with love toward them.″

رَّبَّنَآ إِنِّيٓ أَسۡكَنتُ مِن ذُرِّيَّتِي بِوَادٍ غَيۡرِ ذِي زَرۡعٍ عِندَ بَيۡتِكَ
ٱلۡمُحَرَّمِ رَبَّنَا لِيُقِيمُواْ ٱلصَّلَوٰةَ فَٱجۡعَلۡ أَفۡـِٔدَةٗ مِّنَ ٱلنَّاسِ
تَهۡوِيٓ إِلَيۡهِمۡ

(*Ibrahim 14:37*)

'Ibrāhīm left his wife Hājar and his only son with a heavy heart. Fearing for the worst, but hoping for the best. He has gone through the tests earlier and he had miracles of Allah′s saving power.

WE HAVE LEARNED:

- 'Ibrāhīm, a son of an idol maker, was made a prophet and messenger by Allah.
- Allah blessed 'Ibrāhīm with a son 'Ismā'īl from his Egyptian wife Hājar.
- Makkah was established because of the sacrifice of Hājar.

DO WE KNOW THESE WORDS?

enraged, *Hikmah*, incline, posterity, sacrifice, uncultivable

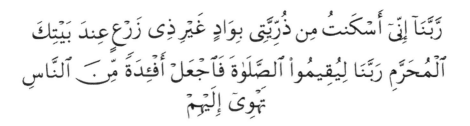

Lesson 10

THE STORY OF THE KA'BAH

After a long time 'Ibrāhīm ﷺ returned to Makkah, fearing the worst but hoping for the best. He was surprised to see a small city growing in the wilderness of the desert. He saw how Allah ﷻ heard his *Du'ā'* and rewarded Hājar for her faith. Makkah was now a town and at the center of it was the well of Zamzam. Hājar told him the story of Zamzam:

> "Soon after you left us, we ran out of food and water. The baby cried and there was no one in sight to help. I ran up the hills of Ṣafā and Marwah to see some signs of life and water but there was desert as far as I could see. But my hope in Allah ﷻ never failed and I believed that He would never let us perish.
>
> Then I saw an angel covering my baby and a spring of water gushing from near his feet. I rushed to the spring and gave water to my child and also quenched my thirst. I called the well 'Zamzam'. Soon after, a stranded caravan of Banū Jarham arrived and decided to stay here with us. Now we have plenty of water and we can grow our own food."

'Ibrāhīm ﷺ was deeply touched by the story of Hājar ﷺ and thanked Allah ﷻ for His Mercy. Now, Allah ﷻ asked him and his son 'Ismā'īl ﷺ to build a House (*Bait Allah*) for Him close to the spring of Zamzam.

'Ibrāhīm ﷺ, 'Ismā'īl ﷺ and the people of Makkah were very happy to see *Bait Allah* standing in their midst. Allah ﷻ asked 'Ibrāhīm ﷺ to declare that *Ḥajj* is an obligation for every believer who can afford to travel to Makkah.

The test for 'Ibrāhīm ﷺ was still not over. Allah ﷻ asked him in a dream to sacrifice his only son 'Ismā'īl ﷺ to Him. Because 'Ibrāhīm ﷺ loved his son dearly, he felt very sad to sacrifice his son to Allah ﷻ with his own hands. However, 'Ibrāhīm ﷺ trusted Allah ﷻ completely, and he loved Him more than any human-- even his own son. He said to himself, "If the Only True God wants this sacrifice then it must be done without hesitation".

He asked his son's opinion. 'Ismā'īl ﷺ had the same unquestioning faith as his father and mother and said immediately, "My father! Do as you have been asked by Allah ﷻ."

'Ibrāhīm ﷺ was strengthened by the firm faith of his son. He quietly prepared to take his son outside Makkah to the valley of Mina to make this sacrifice away from the sight of the people.

As 'Ibrāhīm laid his son down and prepared the knife, suddenly a voice stopped him, saying, "Your sacrifice has been accepted."

Allah ﷻ sent to 'Ibrāhīm a lamb to be slaughtered in place of the boy. Allah ﷻ loved this act of 'Ibrāhīm ﷺ and his son so much that He made this sacrifice part of the rituals of *Ḥajj* and *'Īd al-'Aḍḥā* (Feast of the Sacrifice).

During *Ḥajj* we go through many steps that were taken by 'Ibrāhīm ﷺ, his son 'Ismā'īl ﷺ and his wife Hājar ؓ.

Allah ﷻ had tested the faith of 'Ibrāhīm and he had passed. Thus 'Ibrāhīm ﷺ and his pious followers were made the leaders of humanity. In *Ḥajj* and in the sacrifice of *'Id Al-'Aḍḥā* we remember him and his family and commit ourselves to remain firm in our faith in Allah ﷻ.

Those who believe and do righteous deeds and perform *Ḥajj* with true faith and sincere repentance know they are the true successors of 'Ibrāhīm.

WE HAVE LEARNED:

- Allah ﷻ accepted the Prayers of 'Ibrāhīm ﷺ and the faith of Hājar ؓ.
- The miracle of the spring of Zamzam made the barren valley of Makkah a small city.
- 'Ibrāhīm ﷺ and 'Ismā'īl ﷺ built the *Ka'bah* and enjoined *Ḥajj* upon people.
- During *Ḥajj* and *'Id al 'Aḍḥā* we commemorate the sacrifice of 'Ismā'īl by slaughtering a lamb or other animal.

DO WE KNOW THESE WORDS?

cultivation, enjoin, heritage, offspring, quenched, repentence, ritual

Lesson 11

HOW TO MAKE ḤAJJ

To make *Ḥajj* to *Bait Allah* at least once in a life-time is a *Farḍ* for every Muslim. The conditions for this *Farḍ* are:

-Be a Muslim
-Be an adult
-Be in control of one's senses
-Be in possession of sufficient resources for making a *Ḥajj*
-Be healthy enough to bear the hardship of the trip

Thus, *Ḥajj* is not a *Farḍ* on children, the mentally handicapped or the financially weak.

Obligatory *Ḥajj* is performed only once in life. If one has performed the *Ḥajj* once, all the later *Ḥajj* become *Nafl*. The *Ḥajj* is performed from the 8th to the 13th of *Dhū al-Ḥijjah.*

Many people who can afford it perform the *'Umrah.* The *'Umrah* could be performed on any day except *Ḥajj* time. An *'Umrah* during *Ḥajj* season is also part of *Ḥajj.*

A woman must be accompanied by her *Maḥram.* A *Maḥram* is a husband or a close relative like a son, a father or a brother.

The *Ḥajj* is an experience that every Muslim desires. It is difficult to learn to make *Ḥajj*. However, we shall explain some important steps of *Ḥajj*. You will learn in greater detail when *Insha' Allah* you make it yourself.

Generally the *Ḥujjāj* (those going on *Ḥajj*) get to Makkah before the official start of the *Ḥajj* to spend some time in prayer and preparation. They also want to visit *Masjid An-Nabi* to perform the *Ṣalah* and offer *Salām* to Rasūl-Allah ﷺ standing at the sight of his grave. However, a visit to the *Masjid* or to the grave of the Prophet is not a *Farḍ* and it is not part of the *Ḥajj.*

For the *Ḥujjāj* who come from abroad, the first part of the *Ḥajj* is the *'Umrah. Ḥujjāj* take baths, visit friends and relatives, and make special *'Adi'yah* before leaving on this most blessed journey.

There are special places around Makkah called *Mīqāt*. A *Ḥājj* must put on *'Iḥrām* from the *Mīqāt*, offer two *Rak'at* for *'Umrah* or *Haj*, make the intention to perform the *Ḥajj*, and say *Talbiyah. Talbiyah* is to say:

Labbaika Allahumma labbaika, "I resond to your call O Allah."

An *'Iḥrām* consists of two unsewn pieces of seamless cloth. One part of it is wrapped around the lower part of the body and the other part is wrapped on the upper part.

For women, the *'Iḥrām* is consistent with the Islamic dress code. She must cover her head and body. She may expose her face, hands and feet.

A *Ḥājj* who puts on *'Iḥrām* is required to avoid many things. He or she should not cut the hair and nails. He or she should not kill a living creature and must avoid perfume and combing the hair.

In general people prefer a white-colored *'Iḥrām*. All the *Ḥujjāj* in *'Iḥrām* look alike. King and commoner, rich and poor, all are dressed alike. All are brothers and sisters in Islam. All of them are equal before Allah ﷻ as they gather in Makkah to follow the steps of Hajarah ﵂, Ibrahim ﵇, Ismail ﵇ and Rasulallah ﷺ.

WE HAVE LEARNED:

- A Muslim who wants to go for *Ḥajj* should be an adult and have enough money to pay for it.
- A woman can go for *Ḥajj* only with her *Maḥram.*
- A *ḥājj* who wears *'Iḥrām* must avoid many things and spend most of his time in prayer.

DO YOU KNOW THESE WORDS?

Ḥājj, *Ḥujjāj*, *'Iḥrām* , sane, *Maḥram*

Lesson 12

PERFORMING THE ḤAJJ: THE ‘UMRAH

There are three ways in which people who come from outside the *Miqat* perform the *Ḥajj*: *Tamattu‘*, Qur’ān and *Ifrad*. We shall discuss here only one form of *Ḥajj* called the *Tamattu‘*. You can read about others at the next level. The *Tamattu‘* means "The Benefit".

In the *Tamattu‘ Ḥajj,* a *Hājj* first puts on *’Iḥrām* for the *’Umrah.* Then he removes it after performing the *’Umrah.* On the 8th day of Dhu al-Hijjah he again puts on *’Iḥrām* for the *Ḥajj.*

Most of the *Hujjāj* who come early make the *’Umrah* first and then remove the *’Iḥrām.* By removing the *’Iḥrām*, they are freed from following its special rules. Most then spend their time praying in the Ka’abah and reading the Qur’ān. A prayer in *Bait Allah* has one hundred thousand more *Thawāb* (reward) than in any other place.

The *’Umrah* has many parts. Here we shall deal with each one of them.

The Ṭawāf:

The *Ṭawāf* means going around the Ka‘bah seven times. The *Ṭawāf* starts from and ends at *Al-Ḥajar Al-’Aswad*, the Black Stone. Every time a *Ḥājj* completes one round of *Ṭawāf* he tries to kiss the *Al-Ḥajar Al-’Aswad* or points with his hands toward it. He continues to say *Du‘a’* during the *Ṭawāf* .

At the Multazam:

After the *Ṭawāf,* a *Ḥājj* makes very special *Du‘a’* at the *Multazam.* The *Multazam* is part of *Ka‘bah* between the *Al-Ḥajar Al-’Aswad* and the gate of the *Ka‘bah.* This is a very special place for the acceptance of prayer.

Nafl at Maqām ’Ibrāhīm:

Maqām ’Ibrāhīm is the place where the footmarks of prophet ’Ibrāhīm ﷺ are preserved. The Hājj performs two Raka‘at at the *Maqām ’Ibrāhīm* or any other place in the *Ḥaram* and makes special *Du‘a’*.

Drinking of Zamzam:

The spring of *Zamzam* is now fully covered, but *Zamzam* water is available everywhere in containers. The *Ḥājj* must drink the water standing and facing the *Ka‘bah.* While drinking the water he or she must pray for an increase in his or her knowledge.

The Sa'y:

The Sa'y means to struggle. *Sa'y* in *Ḥajj* or *'Umrah* is a brisk walk between the hills of *Ṣafa* and *Marwah* seven times. The *Ḥājj* must start the *Sa'y* from the *Ṣafa* and must have the intention to make the *Sa'y* before starting it.

Ḥalq or *Taqṣīr*:

At the end of the seventh round which ends at *Marwah*, the *Ḥājj* performs either *Ḥalq* (shaving of the head) or *Taqṣīr* (shortening the hair). A women cannot perform *Ḥalq*. She must have *Taqṣīr*.

Now the *'Umrah* is complete. The *Ḥājj* can remove the *'Iḥrām* and wait for the 8th day of *Dhū al-Ḥijjah* to put on the *'Iḥrām* of the *Ḥajj*. If the *Ḥājj* arrives in Makkah early, he or she must spend the rest of his or her time offering regular and *Nafl* prayers, performing *Nafl Ṭawāf*, making the *Dhikr* and reciting the Qur'ān.

WE HAVE LEARNED:

- Every *Ḥājj* must put on *'Iḥrām* for *Ḥajj* from the *Miqat*
- The *'Umrah* has many parts: the *Ṭawāf* from the *Miqat*, prayer at *Multazam*, two *Sunnah* at *Maqām 'Ibrāhīm*, drinking *Zamzam* water, *Sa'y* and *Ḥalq* or *Taqṣīr*.
- In *Ḥajj Tamattu'* a *Ḥājj* takes off his or her *'Iḥrām* after the *'Umrah* and puts it on again on the 8th of *Dhū al-Ḥijjah* for the *Ḥajj*.

DO WE KNOW THESE WORDS?

Al-Ḥajar Al-'Aswad, Maqām 'Ibrāhīm, Multazim, Tamattu', Qir ān, 'Ifrad, Sa'y, Ḥalq, Taqṣīr.

Lesson 13

PERFORMING THE ḤAJJ: THE COMPLETION

To Mina:

On the eighth day of *Dhū al-Ḥijjah*, the *Ḥujjāj* put on the *'Iḥrām* once again for the *Ḥajj*. Then they go to stay in Mina. Mina is a valley about three miles from Makkah. It is preferable to live in a tent while in Mina.

From Mina to 'Arafāt:

On the ninth of *Dhū al-Ḥijjah,* the *Ḥājj* leaves for the valley of 'Arafāt. Before *Maghrib* on this day, if one is in the valley of 'Arafāt in the condition of *'Ihrām*, and has made the intention of *Ḥajj*, then the main requirement for *Ḥajj* has been fulfilled.

It is in 'Arafāt that Rasūl-Allāh ﷺ gave *Khutbah al-Wada'*, his Last Sermon from *Jabal ar-Raḥmah*, the "Mount of Mercy". The *Khutbah al-Wada'* is one of the most important declarations in human history.

In the plain of 'Arafāt the *Ḥujjāj* stay all day until sunset and spend all their time in prayer and reading the Qur'ān.

From 'Arafāt to Muzdalifah:

Soon after sunset the *Ḥujjāj* leave for the valley of Muzdalifah which is located between Mina and 'Arafāt. At Muzdalifah the *Ḥujjāj* offer *Maghrib* and *'Ishā'* prayers together. They spend the night in the open field.

They go into nearby hills and fields to collect forty nine pebbles from there. For the next three days they will throw stones at the *Jamarāt*. There are three *Jamarāt*.

The *Jamarāt* represent the *Shayātīn*, the Satans. In stoning the *Jamarāt*, a *Ḥājj* rejects Satan and declares his or her firm faith in the One God.

From Muzdalifah back to Mina:

Soon after *Fajr* prayer the *Ḥujjāj* leave for Mina. They go to stone *Jamrah al-'Aqbah*, the First *Jamrah. Jamrah al-'Aqbah* represents the most powerful *Shaiṭān*.

The *Ḥujjāj* must sacrifice an animal. After the sacrifice, they perform *Ḥalq* or *Taqṣīr* and remove the *'Iḥrām*. They take baths and change into their regular clothes.

The *Ṭawāf* of *Ziyārah*:

The next two days (11th and 12th of Dhu al-Hijjah) they will stay in Mina and go out to stone all three *Jamarāt*. Between the 10th and the 12th, the *Ḥujjāj* must go to Makkah and make the *Ṭawāf az-Ziyārah*, The "*Ṭawāf* of the Visit."

Back to Makkah:

Most *Ḥujjāj* return to Makkah on the 12th. Those who stay an extra day must stone the Jamarāt on the 13th as well before leaving.

The *Ḥujjāj* return to Makkah and prepare to leave for the *Ziyārah* of Madinah. Those who have visited Madinah earlier get ready to leave for home. They spend their remaining time mostly in the *Masjid al-Ḥarām* and make additional *Ṭawāf* and prayers.

Rasūl-Allāh ﷺ said:

> "He/she who performed Hajj for the sake of Allah and neither behave in an obscene manner nor act immorally, will revert to (the purity of) the day of his/her birth."
> (al-Bukhari, Ahmad, An-Nisa'i)

WE HAVE LEARNED:

- The *Ḥujjāj* make *Ḥajj* between the 8th and 13th of *Dhu al-Ḥijjah.*
- Staying in the plains of 'Arafāt on the 9th of *Dhu al-Ḥijjah* is the main part of the *Ḥajj.*
- The *Khutbah al-Wadā'* of Rasūl-Allāh ﷺ is one of the most important sermons of human history.

DO WE KNOW THESE WORDS?

'Arafāt, Khutbah al-Wadā', Jamarāt, Ṭawāf az-Ziyārah, Ziyārah, Shaytān, Shayātīn, Jamarah (a)l-'Aqabah

Lesson 14

THE ZIYĀRAH OF MADĪNAH

Almost all the *Ḥujjāj* visit *Al-Madinah al-Munawwarah* the "Illuminated City" of our Prophet Muḥammad ﷺ. A visit to Madīnah is not a necessary part of *Ḥajj*; it is made out of love. Madīnah is the second holiest city in Islam. It is also a *Ḥaram*, a Sacred Place, like Makkah.

Rasūl-Allāh ﷺ said that:

" There are three *Masājid* that one could make special intention and preparations to visit: The Sacred Masjid (Makkah) and the *Masjid al-Aqsa'* (Jerusalem). this *Masjid* of mine (*Al-Masjid an-Nabi*),
(Agreed Upon)

For offering prayer in the *Masjid an-Nabi* one obtains many times the *Thawāb* (reward) of a normal prayer. Many *Ḥujjāj* spend eight days in Madinah and complete forty prayers in the *Masjid* with *Jama'ah*. Rasūl-Allāh ﷺ said:

"Whoever comes and offers forty prayers with consecutively in my Masjid without missing a prayer in between will receive protection from the fire of hell and other punishments and against hypocracy"
(Al-Targhib, Musnad Ahmed)

An important purpose of visiting the Madinah for the Hujjaj is to visit the grave of Rasūl-Allah ﷺ and offer *Salām* to him, thus exhibiting the love of the *Ummah* for their Prophet ﷺ.

People stand up before the grave of Rasūlullāh ﷺ and say:

Assalamu`Alai-ka Ya Rasūlullāh
"Peace be unto you O Messenger of Allah."

The thought of being in the presence of Rasūlullāh ﷺ is so strong that most people can not resist tears and cry openly. Being in Madinah and offering the Salah at the Masjid, as well as offering Salam at the grave of Rasūlullāh ﷺ, is one of the most beautiful experiences of life.

Rasūlullāh ﷺ spent the last ten years of his life in Madinah. There are many places in Madinah which relate to events in the life of Rasūlullāh ﷺ. Many Hujjaj visit

them to relive the experiences of Rasulullah ﷺ and his Sahabah ؓ.
Next to Rasulullah ﷺ are buried his two Sahabah and Khulafa′, Abu Bakr ؓ and Umar ؓ. The Hujjaj offer Salam to these two as they do on the grave of Rasulullah ﷺ.

Very close to the Masjid is Jannat al-Baqi, the graveyard of Madinah. Many members of the family of Rasulullah ﷺ, thousands of Sahabah and many other pious Muslims are buried in the Jannat al-Baqi′.

In the outskirts of Madinah is located Masjid Quba′ the first Masjid of Islam, first built by Rasulullah ﷺ and his Sahabah. To offer two Rakat of the Salah at Masjid Quba′ one gets the Thawab of one Umrah (according to some traditions).

There is also Masjid al-Qiblatain, the Masjid which has two Qiblahs. It commemorates an important event in the life of Rasulullah ﷺ. The Muslims used to pray facing Bait al-Maqdas (in Jerusalem). Once Rasulullah ﷺ was offering the Salah in Jamaah at this Masjid, and he received the Wahi to turn towards the *Kaabah* for Qiblah. Rasulullah ﷺ turned himself from the Qiblah of Bait al-Maqdas to the Qiblah of Bait Allah and the entire Jamaah turned with him. Thus the Masjid is called Qiblatain (two Qiblahs).

Under the mount of Uhud is the field upon which the battle of Uhud was fought in the third year of the Hijrah (A.H.). The graveyard of the Shuhada′ of Uhud is also located there. Hamzah ؓ, the uncle of Rasulullah ﷺ, is buried there.

There are Sabah Masajid (Seven Mosques) built at the grounds where the Battle of the Ditch was fought in 5 A.H.

The Hujjaj visit all these places out of love for Rasulullah ﷺ and his Sahabah ؓ, although these Ziyarat are not part of the Hajj. It is a journey of love that every believing Muslim yearns to undertake.

WE HAVE LEARNED:

- Most of the Hujjaj visit Madinah.
- In Madinah they offer the Salah in the Masjid, give Salam to RasulAllah ﷺ and visit other important places.
- A visit to Madinah is not part of the Hajj, but it shows the love of the Ummah for their Prophet ﷺ.

DO WE KNOW THESE WORDS?

Al-Munawwarah, Bait al-Maqdas, Masjid Qiblatain, Sabah Masajid, Shuhada′.

Lesson 15

JIHAD I: STRUGGLE WITH WEALTH AND WITH PERSONS

According to some scholars Jihad is also a Rukn, a Pillar, of Islam. Everyone agrees that Jihad is one of the most important duties in Islam and it is a Fard on every Muslim.

Jihad as a concept is one of the most misunderstood Islamic concepts. It is commonly translated as ″holy war″. It is understood by many non-Muslims as a war of Muslims against all non-Muslims. Nothing could be further from the truth.

Islam in its meaning and message is a religion of peace and teaches us to live with other human beings in justice, decency, and peace. We are also required to cooperate with everyone in doing those things that are beneficial to the entire society. Islam does not allow the Muslims to hurt, much less kill, other innocent human beings.

Jihad, however, has many meanings and one of its meanings is war. Jihad as war is an organized and well-directed activity that has its own rules and regulations. Every fight of a Muslim against a non-Muslim is not a Jihad. Even under Islamic law, a Muslim would be punished if he does any injustice to a non-Muslim.

The meaning of Jihad must be understood in each situation in which it is used. In this chapter and the next we shall deal with various meanings of Jihad.

Jihad literally means the struggle. And as a struggle can be of various forms, so also can a Jihad be of various forms. The Qur'ān enjoins upon us struggle of every kind. Jihad means struggle and striving in the way of Allah ﷻ. Struggle and striving involves making a very special effort. The Qur'ān commands us:

وَجَٰهِدُواْ فِي ٱللَّهِ حَقَّ جِهَادِهِۦۚ هُوَ ٱجۡتَبَىٰكُمۡ وَمَا جَعَلَ
عَلَيۡكُمۡ فِي ٱلدِّينِ مِنۡ حَرَجٖۚ

″And make Jihad (struggle) for the sake of Allah as much as must be made; He has chosen you and has made no difficulties for you in religion....″
(′Al-Hajj 22:78)

Muslims are enjoined to struggle (make Jihad) in the way of Allah as much as possible. Islam requires of us to make every sacrifice for the pleasure of Allah ﷻ. Allah ﷻ promises support and help for those who struggle in His cause:

وَٱلَّذِينَ جَٰهَدُوا۟ فِينَا لَنَهْدِيَنَّهُمْ سُبُلَنَا ۚ وَإِنَّ ٱللَّهَ لَمَعَ ٱلْمُحْسِنِينَ

Those who make Jihad for Our cause,
We will certainly guide them to Our Path...."
(Al-Ankabut 29:69)

In the Qur'an, making Jihad in the way of Allah is a sign of a true believer:

إِنَّمَا ٱلْمُؤْمِنُونَ ٱلَّذِينَ ءَامَنُوا۟ بِٱللَّهِ وَرَسُولِهِۦ ثُمَّ لَمْ يَرْتَابُوا۟
وَجَٰهَدُوا۟ بِأَمْوَٰلِهِمْ وَأَنفُسِهِمْ فِى سَبِيلِ ٱللَّهِ ۚ أُو۟لَٰٓئِكَ هُمُ
ٱلصَّٰدِقُونَ ﴿١٥﴾

"Those are true Believers, who have believed in Allah and in His Messenger and never since doubted, then made jihad (struggled), with their wealth and with their persons in the path of Allah. Such are the Truthful ones."
('Al-Hujur t 49:15)

The above Ayah describes a true believer as one who believes, does not doubt and makes personal as well as financial Jihad. The Jihad with wealth (Mal) is to spend in the way of Allah ﷻ as much as we can. One way of doing this is through the Zakah which Muslims are required to pay each year. The Zakah is a Fard and the minimum amount that a believer must pay. In addition to the Zakah we must pay Sadaqah and give Hadayah (gifts) and take care of our other social responsibilities. The Jihad of wealth requires us to give to the Islamic cause our maximum financial support.

The personal Jihad requires us to devote all our time, energies and effort for the pleasure of Allah ﷻ. In Islam, working to care for one's family needs is also a Jihad. In fact, our family responsibilities have priority over our Jihad.

Once someone asked the permission of Rasulullah ﷺ to join for the Jihad. Rasulullah ﷺ asked him, "Do you have parents to serve?"
He replied, "Yes, O Messenger of Allah, I have old parents whom I care for."
Rasulullah ﷺ advised him,"Make Jihad by serving them." (Al-Bukhari)

For women, Rasulullah ﷺ stated that Hajj is a perfect Jihad (An-Nasa'i).

WE HAVE LEARNED:

- Jihad means to struggle in the way of Allah ﷻ with one's wealth and person.
- To work for one's family and social responsibilities is also a Jihad in Islam.
- A true believer must devote all his or her resources and time to the cause of Islam.

DO WE KNOW THESE WORDS?

concept, devote, energies, Jihad, Hadayah

Lesson 16

JIHAD II: FIGHTING IN THE WAY OF ALLAH

One of the meanings of Jihad (Struggle) is to struggle in the way of Allah against the enemies of Islam and Muslims. This Jihad is not a random fight against non-Muslims but a struggle to defend Muslims and Islamic interests. In fact, Islam gives full rights to oppressed people to rise against the oppressor for the defense of their rights.
The Qur′an permits the Muslims clearly:

أُذِنَ لِلَّذِينَ يُقَٰتَلُونَ بِأَنَّهُمْ ظُلِمُوا۟ ۚ وَإِنَّ ٱللَّهَ عَلَىٰ نَصْرِهِمْ لَقَدِيرٌ ﴿٣٩﴾ ٱلَّذِينَ
أُخْرِجُوا۟ دِيَٰرِهِم بِغَيْرِ حَقٍّ إِلَّآ أَن يَقُولُوا۟ رَبُّنَا ٱللَّهُ ۗ وَلَوْلَا دَفْعُ ٱللَّهِ ٱلنَّاسَ
بَعْضَهُم بِبَعْضٍ لَّهُدِّمَتْ صَوَٰمِعُ وَبِيَعٌ وَصَلَوَٰتٌ وَمَسَٰجِدُ يُذْكَرُ فِيهَا ٱسْمُ ٱللَّهِ
كَثِيرًا ۗ وَلَيَنصُرَنَّ ٱللَّهُ مَن يَنصُرُهُۥٓ ۗ إِنَّ ٱللَّهَ لَقَوِىٌّ عَزِيزٌ ﴿٤٠﴾

To those against whom war is made permission is given (to defend themselves) because they are wronged, and Indeed Allah is Most-Powerful to give them victory. They (the oppressed) are those who have been expelled from their homes in violation of their right--(for no reason) except that they say, ″Our Lord is Allah.″
(Al-Hajj 22:39-40)

The above ayah emphasizes two points:

First, the permission to make Jihad is given to Muslims when they are oppressed.

Second, the unjustified expulsion of Muslims, in this case from Makkah, justifies the Muslims to wage Jihad against the oppressor.

Waging a war against other people is a serious responsibility and Muslims are not allowed to fight others for no reason. Besides, the Jihad as war is a very organized and controlled activity. Even when waging a war, Muslims must respect the limits set by Allah سُبْحَانَهُ وَتَعَالَىٰ:

وَقَٰتِلُوا۟ فِى سَبِيلِ ٱللَّهِ ٱلَّذِينَ يُقَٰتِلُونَكُمْ
وَلَا تَعْتَدُوٓا۟ ۚ إِنَّ ٱللَّهَ لَا يُحِبُّ ٱلْمُعْتَدِينَ ﴿١٩٠﴾

Fight in the cause of Allah those who fight against you, but do not pass the limits. Indeed Allah does not love those who pass the limits.
(Al-Baqarah 2:190)

However, when it is necessary to fight, the Muslims are required to fight, keeping in mind that they are not fighting against innocent people but against the oppressors:

وَمَا لَكُمْ لَا تُقَٰتِلُونَ فِى سَبِيلِ ٱللَّهِ وَٱلْمُسْتَضْعَفِينَ مِنَ ٱلرِّجَالِ وَٱلنِّسَآءِ وَٱلْوِلْدَٰنِ ٱلَّذِينَ
رَبَّنَآ أَخْرِجْنَا مِنْ هَٰذِهِ ٱلْقَرْيَةِ ٱلظَّالِمِ أَهْلُهَا وَٱجْعَل لَّنَا مِن لَّدُنكَ وَلِيًّا يَقُولُونَ

And why should you not fight in the cause of Allah and of those who, being weak, are ill treated--men, women and children-whose cry (to Allah) is "Our Lord! save us from this town whose people are oppressors; and raise for us from you one who will protect us."
(An-Nisa' 4:75)

Fighting in itself is not the objective of Muslims and they are enjoined to be ready to make peace if others are willing to make peace:

وَإِن جَنَحُواْ لِلسَّلْمِ فَٱجْنَحْ لَهَا وَتَوَكَّلْ عَلَى ٱللَّهِ ۚ

And if they (the enemy) want peace then you also offer them peace and trust in Allah...
(Al-'Anfal 8:61)

If Muslims gain victory during Jihad, they must know that it is not through their own strengths or sacrifices but through the kindness of Allah. They should not feel proud of their achievements or mistreat the enemy. The Qur'an describes the correct Muslim conduct in victory:

ٱلَّذِينَ إِن مَّكَّنَّٰهُمْ فِى ٱلْأَرْضِ أَقَامُواْ ٱلصَّلَوٰةَ وَءَاتَوُاْ ٱلزَّكَوٰةَ
وَأَمَرُواْ بِٱلْمَعْرُوفِ وَنَهَوْاْ عَنِ ٱلْمُنكَرِ ۗ وَلِلَّهِ عَٰقِبَةُ ٱلْأُمُورِ ﴿٤١﴾

...those who, if We give them power in the land, establish the Salah, and pay the Zakah and enjoin what is right and forbid what is wrong. And with Allah rests the final decision of all things.
(Al-Hajj 22:41)

WE HAVE LEARNED:

- Allah ﷻ allows fighting against those who oppress others.
- The Muslims must be ready to offer peace if the enemy is ready to make peace.
- When victorious, the Muslims are required to establish a system of justice and righteousness.

DO WE KNOW THESE WORDS?

oppressed, righteous, violation

Lesson 17

JIHAD III: THE STRUGGLE WITHIN THE SELF

The most important Jihad according to Rasulullah ﷺ is the Jihad an-Nafs (Pronounced as Jihadu-(a)n-Nafs), the Struggle of the Self. It is a personal Jihad with ourselves to fight bad habits and to develop good character.

Jihad an-Nafs prepares us to do those things which Allah ﷻ wants us to do, though we may find them hard or unappealing. Jihad an-Nafs means not to do those things that Allah ﷻ does not want us to do, though we may find pleasure in doing them. Rasulullah ﷺ said:

"The road to Jannah is surrounded by those things that are unpleasant and road to Jahannam is covered by those things that are pleasant."

Jihad an-Nafs prepares us to choose the road to Jannah. In doing *Jihad an-Nafs* a Believer first has firm faith, then he or she gives up bad habits and starts following Islamic Shari'ah. Jihad an-Nafs not only prepares us for a truly Islamic life, but slowly makes it a pleasure for us to lead a pure, simple and pious life.

In Islam the most important thing is the intention. Rasulullah ﷺ said:

Indeed! One's actions are determined by the intention.

For everyone there is a reward for what one intends for.
(Al-Bukhari)

The intention is based upon our inner feelings and thoughts. Jihad an-Nafs gives us the purity of intention and pleasure in righteous actions.

Allah ﷻ says that our intention and inner feelings are as important to Him as our external actions. If our intention is impure, all our actions, however noble, will be of no avail. The Qur'an tells us in relation to the sacrifice we make during the Hajj:

Their flesh and their blood does not reach Allah
but the sincere devotion (Taqwa) from you reaches Him.
(Al-Hajj 22:37)

Now we must understand why the Jihad an-Nafs is the most important Jihad for us. It prepares us spiritually and morally for all other kinds of Jihad in life. It prepares us to sacrifice our life if need be, but it also restrains us from doing injustice against others.

The faith of the non-Muslims is an affair between them and Allah ﷻ. Muslims have a responsibility to give Dàwah in the wisest and most beautiful manner. The guidance is in the hands of Allah ﷻ. Muslims are constantly reminded to do justice in every situation:

O you who believe! Stand out firmly for Allah's witness to fair dealing; and let not the

يَٰٓأَيُّهَا ٱلَّذِينَ ءَامَنُوا۟ كُونُوا۟ قَوَّٰمِينَ لِلَّهِ
شُهَدَآءَ بِٱلْقِسْطِ ۖ وَلَا يَجْرِمَنَّكُمْ شَنَـَٔانُ قَوْمٍ عَلَىٰٓ
أَلَّا تَعْدِلُوا۟ ۚ ٱعْدِلُوا۟ هُوَ أَقْرَبُ لِلتَّقْوَىٰ ۖ وَٱتَّقُوا۟ ٱللَّهَ ۚ إِنَّ
ٱللَّهَ خَبِيرٌۢ بِمَا تَعْمَلُونَ ﴿٨﴾

hatred of others to you make you turn to wrong doing and move away from justice. Be Just: that is next to Taqwa (righteousness). And Allah is well acquainted with what you do.
('Al-Ma'idah 5:8)

WE HAVE LEARNED:

- Rasulullah ﷺ said, The Jihad an-Nafs, "Struggle of the Self" is the most important Jihad in life.
- *Jihad an-Nafs* prepares us for all other kinds of Jihad.
- *Jihad an-Nafs* makes it a pleasure for us to follow Islamic *Shariah*.

DO WE KNOW THESE WORDS?

Dàwah, Jihad an-Nafs, Islamic *Shariah*, witness

Lesson 18

ISLAMIC SHARĪ'AH

Islamic *Sharìah* is a vast field of study and has special experts who spend their lifetime in its study and teaching. Islamic *Sharìah* is a complete way of life. *Sharìah,* literally means an unlimited source of water. Islamic Sharìah, therefore, is an unlimited source of guidance to the laws of Allah ﷻ.

The *Qur'ān* and Sunnah have clearly defined Islamic law and way of life and the Muslims are required to follow their guidance. The Qur'an clearly describes the responsibility of the believers to follow the Qur'an and the Sunnah:

وَمَا كَانَ لِمُؤْمِنٍ وَلَا مُؤْمِنَةٍ إِذَا قَضَى ٱللَّهُ وَرَسُولُهُۥٓ أَمْرًا أَن يَكُونَ
لَهُمُ ٱلْخِيَرَةُ مِنْ أَمْرِهِمْ ۗ وَمَن يَعْصِ ٱللَّهَ وَرَسُولَهُۥ فَقَدْ ضَلَّ ضَلَـٰلًا مُّبِينًا

"It is not for any believing man or woman when Allah and His Messenger have decided a matter, to have any other choice in their affairs...."
(Al-Aḥzāb 33: 36)

Islamic *Sharìah* consists of a wide variety of subjects. All the Islamic laws are not of the same degree of importance; there are questions of *Ḥalāl* (Lawful), *Ḥarām* (Forbidden) and *Mubāḥ* (Permissble). Each one of these is further divided into many other categories.

In order to be fully understood, the Islāmic *Sharìah* requires previous knowledge of many subjects. Hundreds of scholars of Islam have spent their lives developing, studying and teaching it.

The science of *Sharìah* is called *Fiqh* and the person who masters it is called a *Faqīh.* The two terms are derived from the Arabic root word *faqaha* meaning to understand. Thus *Fiqh* is the science of the study of *Sharìah*, and *Faqih* is the scholar of this science. The *Fiqh* and the *Sharìah* in general use have become synonymous. They both mean the science of rules of Islamic teachings, laws and regulations.

To become a *Faqīh* is the greatest merit for a Muslim. There is no better vocation for a Muslim than to study Islamic *Sharìah* and then impart his or her knowledge to others. A *Faqīh,* however, has to go through a long course of study in order to develop a great proficiency in it.

The knowledge of Arabic is, no doubt, a necessary key to understanding Shari`ah. Arabic is a very rich and systematic language. Allah ﷻ has chosen it for imparting His final message and it is important for all Muslims to strive to acquire the knowledge of Arabic language and literature.

The first subject of study is the Qur′an itself. The Qur′an must be understood first, as it was understood by the Sahabah and the earlier generations. Many scholars have written Tafsir (interpretation) of the Qur′an to explain its meaning and message. In fact, to study, teach and interpret one needs a specialization in Qur′anic Studies. A specialist in the Qur′anic study is called a Mufassir. A Mufassir is one who is capable of making Tafsir of the Qur′an.

The second subject of study is the Sunnah of Rasulullah ﷺ. The Sunnah is now compiled in major works of Ahadith. Earlier scholars have developed a detailed `Ilm al-Hadith (the Science of the Hadith). A long tradition of the study, understanding, interpretation and teaching of the Hadith continues from the time of Rasulullah ﷺ until today. A scholar of Hadith is called a Muhaddith.

The Sirah of Rasulullah ﷺ, the life and times of the Sahabah and earlier generations of Muslims, general ancient history, as well as history of religion are all important subjects for a Faqih to master.

The Science of Fiqh (Usul al-Fiqh) is also a very developed field of study. The Usul al-Fiqh deals with the principles and rules of understanding Fiqh. A Faqih must know both Usul al-Fiqh and Fiqh thoroughly.

There are many other subjects that must be studied in order to truly understand Fiqh and Islamic Shari`ah. An Islamic Scholar must also understand modern situations and the new ideas of the times.

WE HAVE LEARNED:

- Islamic Shari`ah is a vast field of study and requires special scholars to study and teach it.
- The knowledge of Arabic, Qur'an, *Sunnah*, *Sirah*, history and many other subnjects is needed for a faqih.
- A Faqih must also understand modern sciences, social situations and new ideas.

DO WE KNOW THESE WORDS?

Fqih, Fiqh, Mufassir, Shariah, Tafsir, 'Ulama', 'Usul al-Fiqh

Lesson 19

ḤALĀL AND ḤARĀM: EARNINGS

Islamic *Sharīah* teaches us that Allāh ﷻ has made certain foods and drinks *Ḥalāl* and certain others *Ḥarām*. In Islam it is also important how we make our earnings. Islamic Sharīah also teaches us which earnings are *Ḥalāl* and which are *Ḥarām*.

Islam enjoins upon everyone to adopt *Ḥalāl* means to earn a living. Jabir ؓ related that *Rasūlullāh* ﷺ said:

"O people! be conscious of your duty to Allāh and do not adopt wrong means of earning. Indeed no one would die unless he has received all his provisions, though it may be delayed. So seek what is *Ḥalāl* and avoid what is *Ḥarām*."
(Ibn Majah)

Rasūlullāh ﷺ taught us that we should never adopt Haram ways of earning. Allah ﷻ has determind everyone's provision and he or she should try to secure it through *Ḥalāl* means. Many people follow *Ḥarām* paths to make themselves rich and to live better lives. In fact they would have gotten whatever Allāh ﷻ had destined for them but they decided to follow the *Ḥarām* path to secure it. *Ḥarām* earnings have no Barakah (Blessings of Allāh) and do not bring us happiness.

Allah ﷻ especially blesses the earnings which are *Ḥalāl*. The *Ḥalāl* earnings are:

Those which one earns by offering his services for a salary or a fee for a *Ḥalāl* sevice.

The profits earned by a *Ḥalāl* business.
Produce and sales from one's land.
Money and property which one rightfully inherits or receives as a gift.

Once *Rasūlullāh* ﷺ was asked,"Which earning is the best?"

He replied, "Acceptable business and the work which one does with one's own labor."
(Mishkāt)

An acceptable business is one which is conducted honestly. A business person is required to be just and fair in his or her dealings. He or she should not over-charge people and must not give them less than their full measure. The Qur'ān advises us:

أَوۡفُواْ ٱلۡكَيۡلَ وَلَا تَكُونُواْ مِنَ ٱلۡمُخۡسِرِينَ ﴿١٨١﴾
وَزِنُواْ بِٱلۡقِسۡطَاسِ ٱلۡمُسۡتَقِيمِ ﴿١٨٢﴾
وَلَا تَبۡخَسُواْ ٱلنَّاسَ أَشۡيَآءَهُمۡ وَلَا تَعۡثَوۡاْ فِي ٱلۡأَرۡضِ مُفۡسِدِينَ ﴿١٨٣﴾

Give full measure and cause no loss (to others by cheating). Weigh with scales true and upright. And withhold not things due to people and do not spread mischief in the land.

('Ash Shu'rā 26:181-183)

Acceptable business also means to trade in those things that are permitted by Allāh ﷻ. Thus unacceptable business deals in those things that are *Ḥarām*. The examples of *Ḥarām* business are:

Producing and selling alchohol and other intoxicants; pork products; bad videos, movies or books; anything forbidden by Islām, etc.

Dealing with usury (making money by loaning money with fixed interest rates).

Earning money in gambling and other games of chance.

Earnings from the services which are forbidden such as fortune telling by any means, magic and sorcery.

Thus Islām has two conditions of *Ḥalāl* earnings; it must be earned through *Ḥalāl* means and it must be earned through honest work.

WE HAVE LEARNED:

- Islamic *Sharīah* enjoins upon us the duty to earn our living in *Ḥalāl* way.
- Islamic *Sharīah* teaches us both what are *Ḥalāl* and *Ḥarām* ways of earnings
- A business is *Ḥalāl* unless it deals in *Ḥarām* products or uses *Ḥarām* methods.

DO WE KNOW THESE WORDS?

Barakah, full measure, intoxicants, provisions, usury

Lesson 20

HALAL AND HARAM: FOOD AND DRINKS

Most of the things that Allah ﷻ has created for us are pure, clean and life giving. We breathe fresh air, we have an abundant supply of water and we have healthy food to eat. All these things support our lives and, if used properly maintain good health.

All the Halal things are permitted for us to use and Allah ﷻ enjoins upon humanity to use them properly:

يَٰٓأَيُّهَا ٱلنَّاسُ كُلُوا۟ مِمَّا فِى ٱلْأَرْضِ حَلَٰلًا طَيِّبًا وَلَا تَتَّبِعُوا۟
خُطُوَٰتِ ٱلشَّيْطَٰنِ ۚ إِنَّهُۥ لَكُمْ عَدُوٌّ مُّبِينٌ ﴿١٦٨﴾

O Humankind! Eat of that which is Halal and pure in the Earth, and follow not the footsteps of the Shaitan, Indeed he is an open enemy to you.
(Al-Baqarah 168)

A Believer is required to use them and show his thankfulness to Allah ﷻ:

يَٰٓأَيُّهَا ٱلَّذِينَ ءَامَنُوا۟ كُلُوا۟ مِن طَيِّبَٰتِ مَا رَزَقْنَٰكُمْ
وَٱشْكُرُوا۟ لِلَّهِ إِن كُنتُمْ إِيَّاهُ تَعْبُدُونَ ﴿١٧٢﴾

O You who believe! Eat of the good things we have provided for you and be thankful to Allah. It is indeed He whom you must worship.
(Al-Baqarah 2:172)

Eating Halal food must make us grateful to Allah ﷻ. It must also guide us to His path.

Just as Allah ﷻ has made Halal the eating of certain foods and drinking of certain drinks, He has made others Haram. Islamic Shariah details that which is Haram. Among the Haram (forbidden) things are:

The meat of an animal which is not slaughtered in the Islamic way of Dhabihah, as is the meat of an animal or bird which is forbidden. The properly slaughtered meat of the People of the Book (Jews and Christians) is permitted but that of a Mushrik (someone who believes in many gods) is not.

Any product that uses any part of a Haram animal (like pigs) is forbidden.
The meat of any already dead animal or bird whether Halal or Haram. (For example, if an animal dies of a disease or is struck by a car, it is Haram to eat it.)
The blood of any animal.
All intoxicating drinks or drugs.
All the things that are Najas, ritually impure such as urine and stool, etc.

Allah ﷻ enjoins upon us to eat and drink and enjoy life but not to ignore the limits set by Allah ﷻ. In buying products from the market we must carefully check the ingredients. The list of ingredients tells us what a product contains. We should specifically check if the shortening is pure vegetable or consists of animal fat.

There are certain eating manners particular to Islam. Washing our hands before eating is extremely important, as are sitting in a clean place and using clean plates and pots. We use the right hand for eating. We do not stand while eating. The Bismillah is said before beginning the meal and we say Al-Hamdu li-llah at meal's end.

Eating together brings special Barakah. It is best to try to eat in the company of our family and friends. We must share our food with those who are less fortunate. In taking a serving we have to show consideration for other people who will be taking after us. We should avoid overeating and leave one third of the stomach empty.

Allah ﷻ has made many things Halal and we must choose between them for reasons of both taste and health. A balanced diet consists of products of meat, dairy, fruits, vegetables and grains. Health is a gift of Allah ﷻ and we must preserve it. Rasulullah ﷺ said:

"Allah ﷻ prefers a strong Believer over a weak Believer."

WE HAVE LEARNED:
- Allah ﷻ has made certain foods and drinks Halal and certain others Haram.
- We must eat and drink that which is Halal and be thankful to Allah ﷻ
- We must follow Islamic manners in eating and drinking.

DO WE KNOW THESE WORDS?
balanced diet, dhabihah, to preserve, People of the Book

APPENDIX I MOST BEAUTIFUL NAMES OF ALLAH

أسماء اللّٰه الحُسنى

هو اللّٰه الذي لا إلٰه إلاَّ هُو

اَللّٰهُ	Allah(u)	Allah = The One God
اَلرَّحْمٰنُ	Ar-Rahman(u)	The Compassionate
اَلرَّحِيمُ	Ar-Rahim(u)	The Merciful
اَلْمَلِكُ	Al-Malik(u)	The King, the Sovereign
اَلْقُدُّوسُ	Al-Quddūs(u)	The Holy
اَلسَّلَامُ	As-Salām(u)	The Author of Safety
اَلْمُؤْمِنُ	Al-Mu'min(u)	The Guardian of Faith, The Giver of Peace
اَلْمُهَيْمِنُ	Al-Muhaimin(u)	The Protector, The Guardian
اَلْعَزِيزُ	Al-'Azīz(u)	The Strong
اَلْجَبَّارُ	Al-Jabbār(u)	The Compeller
اَلْمُتَكَبِّرُ	Al-Mutakabbir(u)	The Majestic
اَلْخَالِقُ	Al-Khāliq(u)	The Creator
اَلْبَارِئُ	Al-Bāri'(u)	The Maker
اَلْمُصَوِّرُ	Al-Muṣawwir(u)	The Fashioner
اَلْغَفَّارُ	Al-Ghaffār(u)	The Great Forgiver
اَلْقَهَّارُ	Al-Qahhār(u)	The Dominant
اَلْوَهَّابُ	Al-Wahhāb(u)	The Bestower
اَلرَّزَّاقُ	Ar-Razzāq(u)	The Sustainer
اَلْفَتَّاحُ	Al-Fattah(u)	The Opener
اَلْعَلِيمُ	Al-'Alīm(u)	The All-Knowing

اَلقَابِضُ	Al-Qabiḍ(u)	The Retainer, the Withholder
اَلبَاسِطُ	Al-Bāsit(u)	The Enlarger, The Grantor
اَلخَافِضُ	Al-K͟hafiḍ(u)	The Abaser
اَلرَّافِعُ	Ar-Rāfi'(u)	The Exalter, The Uplifter
اَلمُعِزُّ	Al-Mu'izz(u)	The Honorer, The Strengthener
اَلمُذِلُّ	Al-Mud͟hill(u)	The Humiliator
اَلسَّمِيعُ	Al-Samī'(u)	The All-Hearing, The Hearer
اَلبَصِيرُ	Al-Baṣīr(u)	The All-Seeing
اَلحَكَمُ	Al-Ḥakam(u)	The Judge
اَلعَدْلُ	Al-'Adl(u)	The Just
اَللَّطِيفُ	Al-Laṭīf(u)	The Subtle, The Gracious
اَلخَبِيرُ	Al-K͟habīr(u)	The Aware
اَلحَلِيمُ	Al-Ḥalīm(u)	The Clement, The Forebearing
اَلعَظِيمُ	Al-'Aẓīm(u)	The Mighty
اَلغَفُورُ	Al-Ghafur(u)	The Forgiving
اَلشَّكُورُ	As͟h-S͟hakūr(u)	The Grateful, The Appreciative
اَلعَلِيُّ	Al-'Aliyy(u)	The High, The Sublime
اَلكَبِيرُ	Al-Kabīr(u)	The Great
اَلحَفِيظُ	Al-Ḥafīẓ(u)	The Preserver, The Protector
اَلمُقِيتُ	Al-Muqīt(u)	The Guardian, The Feeder, The Sustainer
اَلحَسِيبُ	Al-Ḥasīb(u)	The Reckoner
اَلجَلِيلُ	Al-Jalīl(u)	The Lofty, The Exalted, The Sublime
اَلكَرِيمُ	Al-Karīm(u)	The Bountiful, The Gracious
اَلرَّقِيبُ	Ar-Raqīb(u)	The Watcher, The Watchful
اَلمُجِيبُ	Al-Mujīb(u)	The Responsive, the Hearkener

اَلْوَاسِعُ	Al-Wāsi'(u)	The Vast, the All-Embracing, The Magnanimous
اَلْحَكِيمُ	Al-Ḥakīm(u)	The Most Wise, The Most Judicious
اَلْوَدُودُ	Al-Wadūd(u)	The Most Loving
اَلْمَجِيدُ	Al-Majīd(u)	The Glorious, The Exalted, The Glorified
اَلْبَاعِثُ	Al-Bā'ith(u)	The Resurrector
اَلشَّهِيدُ	Ash-Shahīd(u)	The Witness
اَلْحَقُّ	Al-Ḥaqq(u)	The Truth, the True
اَلْوَكِيلُ	Al-Wakīl(u)	The Trustee
اَلْقَوِيُّ	Al-Qawiyy(u)	The Strong
اَلْمَتِينُ	Al-Matīn(u)	The Firm
اَلْوَلِيُّ	Al-Waliyy(u)	The Protecting Friend
اَلْحَمِيدُ	Al-Hamīd(u)	The Praiseworthy
اَلْمُحْصِي	Al-Muḥṣi	The Counter
اَلْمُبْدِئُ	Al-Mubdi'(u)	The Originator
اَلْمُعِيدُ	Al-Mu'īd(u)	The Reproducer
اَلْمُحْيِي	Al-Muḥyī	The Restorer, the Giver of Life
اَلْمُمِيتُ	Al-Mumīt(u)	The Destroyer, The Determiner of Death
اَلْحَيُّ	Al-Hayy(u)	The Alive
اَلْقَيُّومُ	Al-Qayyūm(u)	The Self-Sustaining
اَلْوَاجِدُ	Al-Wājid(u)	The Perceiver, The Finder
اَلْوَاحِدُ	Al-Wāḥid(u)	The One
اَلصَّمَدُ	Aṣ-Ṣamad(u)	The Independent
اَلْقَادِرُ	Al-Qādir(u)	The Capable, The Potent, The Powerful
اَلْمُقْتَدِرُ	Al-Muqtadir(u)	The Dominant, The Posseser of Power and Strength
اَلْمُقَدِّمُ	Al-Muqaddim(u)	The Promoter, The Giver, The Donor

اَلْمُؤَخِّرُ	Al-Mu'a khir(u)	The Delayer
اَلأَوَّلُ	Al-'Awwal(u)	The First
اَلآخِرُ	Al-'Ākhir(u)	The Last
اَلظَّاهِرُ	Aẓ-Ẓahir(u)	The Manifest
اَلْبَاطِنُ	Al-Baṭin(u)	The Hidden
اَلْوَالِي	Al-Wāliy(u)	The Governor
اَلْمُتَعَالِي	Al-Muta'ālī	The High, The Exalted
اَلْبَرُّ	Al-Barr(u)	The Righteous, The Kind, The Pious
اَلتَّوَّابُ	At-Tawwab(u)	The Forgiving, The Merciful
اَلْعَفُوُّ	Al-'Afuww(u)	The Forgiver, The Pardoner
اَلْمُنْتَقِمُ	Al-Muntaqim(u)	The Avenger
اَلرَّؤُوفُ	Ar-Ra'ūf(u)	The Compassionate, The Benevolent, The Gracious
مَالِكُ اَلْمُلْكِ	Maliku (a)l-Mulki	The Owner of Sovereignty
ذُو اَلْجَلاَلِ وَٱلإِكْرَامِ	Dhu (a)l-Jalāli wa-(a)l-Ikrām(i)	The Lord of Majesty and Bounty
اَلْمُقْسِطُ	Al-Muqsit(u)	The Equitable, The Just, The Fair
اَلْجَامِعُ	Al-Jāmi'(u)	The Gatherer, the Collector
اَلْغَنِيُّ	Al-Ghaniyy(u)	The Self-Sufficient
اَلْمُغْنِي	Al-Mughni	The Enricher
اَلْمُعْطِي	Al-Mu'ṭī	The Bestower, the Giver
اَلْمَانِعُ	Al-Māni'(u)	The Withholder
اَلنَّافِعُ	An-Nāfi'(u)	The Propitious, The Beneficial, The Salutary
اَلضَّارُّ	Ad-Dārr(u)	The Distresser
اَلنُّورُ	An-Nūr(u)	The Light
اَلْهَادِي	Al-Hādi	The Guide
اَلْبَدِيعُ	Al-Badī'(u)	The Incomparable

اَلبَاقِي	Al-Bāqī	The Everlasting
اَلوَارِثُ	Al-Wārith(u)	The Heir, The Inheriter
اَلرَّشِيدُ	Ar-Rashīd(u)	The Guide to the Right Path, The Discerning, The Reasonable, The Rational
اَلصَّبُورُ	Aṣ-Ṣabūr(u)	The Most Patient

BEAUTIFUL NAMES OF GOD IN ARABIC

APPENDIX II Selected ‘*Ad’iyah* for *Tawaf* of *Ka’bah*

NOTE: There are no prescribed or recommended *Ad‘iyah* for the *Tawaf* of *Ka‘bah* except one to be recited between the Yemenite angle and the Black Stone angle (see below). The *Ad‘iyah* are selected by pious Muslims and are based upon Qur’an and *Sunnah*. We recommend that these be memorized and recited after the *Salah*.

Du'a For the First Round

دُعَاءُ الشَّوْطِ الأَوَّلْ

سُبْحَانَ اللهِ وَالحَمْدُ لِلهِ وَلاَ اِلَهَ إِلاَّ اللهُ وَاللهُ اَكْبَرُ وَلاَ حَوْلَ وَلاَ قُوَّةَ إِلاَّ بِاللهِ العَلِيِّ العَظِيمِ،
وَالصَّلٰوةُ وَالسَّلاَمُ عَلٰى رَسُولِ اللهِ صَلَّى اللهُ عَلَيْهِ وَسَلَّمَ، اَللّٰهُمَّ اِيمَانًا بِكَ وَتَصْدِيقًا بِكِتَابِكَ
وَوَفَاءً بِعَهْدِكَ وَاتِّبَاعًا لِسُنَّةِ نَبِيِّكَ وَحَبِيبِكَ مُحَمَّدٍ صَلَّى اللهُ عَلَيْهِ وَسَلَّم ، اَللّٰهُمَّ اِنِّي اَسْاَلُكَ
العَفْوَ وَالعَافِيَةَ وَالمُعَافَاةَ الدَّائِمَةَ فِي الدِّينِ وَالدُّنْيَا وَالاٰخِرَةِ، وَالفَوْزَ بِالجَنَّةِ وَالنَّجَاةَ مِنَ النَّارِ.

(ويقول بين الركنين في كل شوط)

رَبَّنَا اٰتِنَا فِي الدُّنْيَا حَسَنَةً وَفِي الاٰخِرَةِ حَسَنَةً وَقِنَا عَذَابَ النَّارِ ، وَاَدْخِلْنَا الجَنَّةَ مَعَ الاَبْرَارِ ، يَا
عَزِيزُ يَا غَفَّارُ ، يَا رَبَّ العَالَمِينَ.

(ويقول أمام الحجر الأسود)

بسم الله ، الله أكبر ، لله الحمد.

Translation:

Glory be to Allāh and all praise is due unto Allāh. And none is worthy of worship except Allah. And Allāh is most great. There is no might, no power but from Allāh the most High, the Great. And blessings and peace be on the Messenger of Allāh.

O Allāh, I am performing this duty with complete faith in You and with belief in the truth of Your Book, and in the fulfillment of my pledge to You, and in the wake of the Tradition of Your Prophet and Your beloved friend Muhammed, may peace and blessings of Allāh be upon him!

O Allāh, I implore You to grant me forgiveness, safety and general pardon in the matters of faith, of this world and the hereafter, and also grant me success leading to Paradise and deliverance from the Fire.

Between the Yemenite angle and the Black Stone angle, the pilgrim recites in each *tawāf*:

O our Lord, give us good in this world and also in the next world, and deliver us from the torment of Hell-fire, and cause us to enter the Garden along with the righteous, O Powerful, O Forgiver, O Lord of all the worlds.

The pilgrim declares as he arrives in front of the Black Stone which he hails:

In the name of God, God is most Great, Praise be God.

Du'a For the Second Round

دُعَاءُ اَلشَّوطُ اَلثَّانِي

اَللّٰهُمَّ إِنَّ هٰذَا البَيْتَ بَيْتُكَ وَالحَرَمَ حَرَمُكَ وَالأَمْنَ اَمْنُكَ وَالعَبْدَ عَبْدُكَ وَابْنُ عَبْدِكَ ، وَهٰذَا مَقَامُ العَائِذِ بِكَ مِنَ النَّارِ، فَحَرِّمْ لُحُومَنَا وَبَشَرَتَنَا عَلَى النَّارِ ، اَللّٰهُمَّ حَبِّبْ اِلَيْنَا الاِيْمَانَ وَزَيِّنْهُ فِي قُلُوبِنَا وَكَرِّهْ اِلَيْنَا الكُفْرَ وَالفُسُوقَ وَالعِصْيَانَ وَاجْعَلْنَا مِنَ الرَّاشِدِيْنَ ، اَللّٰهُمَّ قِنِي عَذَابَكَ يَوْمَ تَبْعَثُ عِبَادَكَ ، اَللّٰهُمَّ ارْزُقْنِي الجَنَّةَ بِغَيْرِ حِسَابٍ.

Translation:

O Allāh, verily this House is Your House and this sanctuary is Your sanctuary, and the peace here is Your peace, and these creatures Your servants. I am Your servant and the son of Your servant. This is an asylum for a person seeking Your refuge from the Fire. For this render our flesh and faces unlawful unto the Fire.

O Allāh, make the faith amiable unto us and prepare the same in our hearts. Render infidelity and iniquity and disobedience hateful unto us, and thereby cause us to walk in the right way.

O Allāh, grant me deliverance from Your chastisement on the day You shall resurrect Your servants. O Allāh, grant me in the Garden provisions superabundantly.

Du'a For the Third Round

دُعَاءُ اَلشَّوطُ اَلثَّالِثُ

اَللّٰهُمَّ اِنِّي اَعُوذُ بِكَ مِنَ الشَّكِّ وَالشِّرْكِ وَالشِّقَاقِ وَالنِّفَاقِ وَسُوءِ الاَخْلَاقِ وَسُوءِ المَنْظَرِ وَالمُنْقَلَبِ فِي المَالِ وَالاَهْلِ وَالوَلَدِ ، اَللّٰهُمَّ اِنِّى اَعُوذُ بِكَ مِنْ فِتْنَةِ القَبْرِ وَاَعُوذُ بِكَ مِنْ فِتْنَةِ المَحْيَا وَالمَمَاتِ .

Translation:

O Allāh, I seek Your refuge from doubt, idolatry, schism, hypocrisy, insincerity, wrong thinking and inversion in respect of property, family and children.

O Allāh, I seek Your pleasure and the bliss of the Garden. I also seek Your refuge from Your anger and the torment of the Fire.

O Allāh, I also seek Your refuge from the trial of the grave and also from the ordeals of life and pangs of death.

Du'a For the Fourth Round

دُعَاءُ الشَّوْطِ الرَّابِعِ

اَللّٰهُمَّ اجْعَلْهُ حَجًّا مَّبْرُوْرًا وَّسَعْيًا مَّشْكُوْرًا وَّذَنْبًا مَّغْفُوْرًا وَّعَمَلاً صَالِحًا مَّقْبُوْلاً وَّتِجَارَةً لَّنْ تَبُوْرَ،
يَا عَالِمَ مَا فِي الصُّدُوْرِ ، اَخْرِجْنِيْ يَا اَللهُ مِنَ الظُّلُمٰتِ اِلَى النُّوْرِ ، اَللّٰهُمَّ اِنِّي اَسْاَلُكَ مُوْجِبَاتِ
رَحْمَتِكَ وَعَزَائِمَ مَغْفِرَتِكَ وَالسَّلَامَةَ مِنْ كُلِّ اِثْمٍ وَالْغَنِيْمَةَ مِنْ كُلِّ بِرٍّ وَ الْفَوْزَ بِالْجَنَّةِ وَالنَّجَاةَ مِنَ
النَّارِ ، رَبِّ قَنِّعْنِي بِمَا رَزَقْتَنِي وَبَارِكْ لِي فِيْمَا اَعْطَيْتَنِي وَاخْلُفْ عَلَيَّ كُلَّ غَائِبَةٍ لِي مِنْكَ بِخَيْرٍ.

<u>Translation:</u>

Allāh, make this for me a righteous pilgrimage and an endeavour acceptable unto You and a means of forgiveness of sin, and also an act that is right and fit, and a merchandise that shall not perish.

O You who knowest the innermost parts of our hearts. Lead me, Oh Allāh, out of the dark into the light.

O Allāh, I implore You to grant me Your mercy and Your forgiveness, and to save me from every type of sin. And grant me an opportunity to reap all good and success leading to Paradise and deliverance from Hell.

O my Lord, make me such that I ever feel contented with what You have bestowed upon me, and grant You bliss in whatever You hast given me.

Du'a For the Fifth Round

دُعَاءُ الشَّوْطِ الْخَامِسِ

اَللّٰهُمَّ اَظِلَّنِي تَحْتَ ظِلِّ عَرْشِكَ يَوْمَ لَا ظِلَّ اِلَّا ظِلُّكَ وَلَا بَاقِيَ اِلَّا وَجْهُكَ، وَاسْقِنِي مِنْ حَوْضِ
نَبِيِّكَ سَيِّدِنَا مُحَمَّدٍ صَلَّى اللهُ عَلَيْهِ وَسَلَّمَ شَرْبَةً هَنِيْئَةً مَرِيْئَةً لَا نَظْمَأُ بَعْدَهَا اَبَدًا ، اَللّٰهُمَّ اِنِّي
اَسْاَلُكَ مِنْ خَيْرِ مَا سَاَلَكَ مِنْهُ نَبِيُّكَ سَيِّدُنَا مُحَمَّدٌ صَلَّى اللهُ عَلَيْهِ وَسَلَّمَ ، وَاَعُوْذُ بِكَ مِنْ شَرِّ
مَا اسْتَعَاذَكَ مِنْهُ نَبِيُّكَ سَيِّدُنَا مُحَمَّدٌ صَلَّى اللهُ عَلَيْهِ وَسَلَّمَ ، اَللّٰهُمَّ اِنِّي اَسْاَلُكَ الْجَنَّةَ وَنَعِيْمَهَا
وَمَا يُقَرِّبُنِي اِلَيْهَا مِنْ قَوْلٍ اَوْ فِعْلٍ اَوْ عَمَلٍ، وَاَعُوْذُ بِكَ مِنَ النَّارِ وَمَا يُقَرِّبُنِي اِلَيْهَا مِنْ قَوْلٍ اَوْ
فِعْلٍ اَوْ عَمَلٍ.

<u>Translation:</u>

O Allāh, take me under the shade of Your Throne on the day when there shall be no shade but Yours, and no survivor but Your face. Quench my thirst from the tank of Your Prophet, our chief Muhammed, may Allāh send blessings and peace upon him, a pleasant and wholesome draught whereafter I shall never again feel thirst.

O Allāh, I ask You for the best that Your Prophet, our chief Muhammed, asked You for. I also seek Your refuge from evil that the Prophet, our chief Muhammed, may Allāh send blessings and peace on him, hath sought.

O Allāh, I implore You to grant me Paradise and its delights and all those things - actions, sayings, or acts - which can bring me nearer unto it.

Du'a For the Sixth Round

دُعَاءُ اَلشَّوطُ اَلسَّادِسْ

اَللّٰهُمَّ اِنَّ لَكَ عَلَيَّ حُقُوقًا كَثِيرَةً فِيمَا بَيْنِي وَبَيْنَكَ، وَحُقُوقًا كَثِيرَةً فِيمَا بَيْنِي وَبَيْنَ خَلْقِكَ

اَللّٰهُمَّ مَا كَانَ لَكَ مِنْهَا فَاغْفِرْهُ، وَمَا كَانَ لِخَلْقِكَ فَتَحَمَّلْهُ عَنِّي وَاغْنِنِي بِحَلاَلِكَ عَنْ حَرَامِكَ،

وَبِطَاعَتِكَ عَنْ مَعْصِيَتِكَ، وَبِفَضْلِكَ عَمَّنْ سِوَاكَ يَا وَاسِعَ الْمَغْفِرَةِ - اَللّٰهُمَّ اِنَّ بَيْتَكَ عَظِيمٌ

وَوَجْهَكَ كَرِيمٌ وَ اَنْتَ يَا اَللّٰهُ حَلِيمٌ كَرِيمٌ عَظِيمٌ، تُحِبُّ الْعَفْوَ، فَاعْفُ عَنِّي.

Translation:

Oh Allāh, I owe You innumerable duties that concern You and me, and innumerable duties also that concern Your creatures and me.

O Allāh, acquit me of my debts towards You and acquit Yourself on my behalf of my duties towards Your creatures.

O Allāh, grant me that which is lawful and preserve me from the unlawful. Grant me the privilege of obedience unto You and save me from disobedience unto You. Grant me Your grace rather that otherwise, O You Forgiver of all things.

O Allāh, Your House is great, Your face is noble and You art, O Allāh, forbearing, Noble the Great. You who lovest forgiveness, forgive me

Du'a For the Seventh Round

دُعَاءُ اَلشَّوطُ اَلسَّابِعْ

اَللّٰهُمَّ اِنِي اَسْاَلُكَ اِيمَانًا كَامِلاً وَيَقِينًا صَادِقًا وَرِزْقًا وَاسِعًا وَقَلْبًا خَاشِعًا وَلِسَانًا ذَاكِرًا وَحَلاَلاً

طَيِّبًا وَتَوْبَةً نَصُوحًا وَتَوْبَةً قَبْلَ الْمَوْتِ وَرَاحَةً عِنْدَ الْمَوْتِ وَمَغْفِرَةً وَرَحْمَةً بَعْدَ الْمَوْتِ وَالْعَفْوَ

عِنْدَ الْحِسَابِ وَالْفَوْزَ بِالْجَنَّةِ وَالنَّجَاةَ مِنَ النَّارِ بِرَحْمَتِكَ يَا عَزِيزُ يَا غَفَّارُ، رَبِّ زِدْنِي عِلْمًا

وَاَلْحِقْنِي بِالصَّالِحِينَ.

Translation:

O Allāh, I implore You to bestow on me perfect faith, sincere belief, boundless provision, a humble heart, a tongue wont to mention Your name, pleasant lawful things, true repentance, an opportunity to express contrition before death and satisfaction at the moment of death, forgiveness and mercy after death and satisfaction at the moment of death, forgiveness and mercy after death, and Your forgiveness on the Day of Judgment.

O You Mighty, O You Merciful and Forgiving, grant me Paradise and preserve me from the Fire.

O my Lord, increase knowledge unto me and join me with the righteous.

Du'a at The Multazim

دُعَاءُ الْمُلْتَزَمُ

اَللّٰهُمَّ يَا رَبَّ الْبَيْتِ الْعَتِيقِ اَعْتِقْ رِقَابَنَا وَرِقَابَ اٰبَآئِنَا وَاُمَّهَاتِنَا وَاِخْوَانِنَا وَاَوْلَادِنَا مِنَ النَّارِ يَا ذَا
الْجُودِ وَالْكَرَمِ وَالْفَضْلِ وَالْمَنِّ وَالْعَطَاءِ وَالْاِحْسَانِ ، اَللّٰهُمَّ اَحْسِنْ عَاقِبَتَنَا فِى الْاُمُورِ كُلِّهَا
وَاَجِرْنَا مِنْ خِزْيِ الدُّنْيَا وَعَذَابِ الْاٰخِرَةِ ، اَللّٰهُمَّ اِنِّي عَبْدُكَ وَابْنُ عَبْدِكَ وَاقِفٌ تَحْتَ بَابِكَ مُلْتَزِمٌ
بِاَعْتَابِكَ مُتَذَلِّلٌ بَينَ يَدَيْكَ اَرْجُو رَحْمَتَكَ وَاَخْشٰى عَذَابَكَ يَا قَدِيمَ الْاِحسَانِ ، اَللّٰهُمَّ اِنِّي اَسْاَلُكَ
اَنْ تَرْفَعَ ذِكْرِي وَتَضَعَ وِزْرِي وَتُصْلِحَ اَمْرِىْ وَتُطَهِّرَ قَلْبِي وَتُنَوِّرَ لِي فِي قَبْرِي وَتَغْفِرَ لِي ذَنْبِي ،
وَاَسْاَلُكَ الدَّرَجَاتِ الْعُلٰى مِنَ الْجَنَّةِ - اٰمِين .

Translation:
O Allāh, O Lord of the ancient House, save us and save our parents, brothers and children for the Fire. O You whose hospitality, generosity, grace and magnanimity are without limits.

O Allāh, make the end of all our affairs noble and grant us refuge from the worldly disgrace and the torment of the hereafter.

O Allāh, I am Your servant and the son of Your servant, standing underneath Your Gate and holding Your thresholds with full humility in Your presence. I hope to receive Your mercy and I dread the torment of Your chastisement. O Thou are Eternal in Your benevolence.

O Allāh, I implore You to raise my mention and to remove from me my burden, to improve my affair, to purify my heart, and to illuminate my grave for me, to pardon my sins and to grant me lofty ranks in the Garden of Paradise. Amen.

Salam to be Recited at the Prophet's Tomb at Madinah

اَلسَّلَامُ وَالصَّلٰوةُ عَلٰى اَلرَّسُول

اَلسَّلَامُ عَلٰى رَسُولِ اللّٰهِ صَلَّى اَللّٰهُ عَلَيْهِ وَسَلَّمَ، اَلسَّلَامُ عَلَيْكَ أَيُّهَا اَلنَّبِيُّ وَرَحْمَةُ اَللّٰهِ وَبَرَكَاتُهُ،
اَلصَّلَاةُ وَالسَّلَامُ عَلَيْكَ يَا سَيِّدَنَا يَا رَسُولَ اَللّٰهِ، اَلصَّلَاةُ وَالسَّلَامُ عَلَيْكَ يَا نَبِيَّ اَللّٰهِ، اَلصَّلَاةُ
وَالسَّلَامُ عَلَيْكَ يَا خَيْرَ خَلْقِ اَللّٰهِ.

Translation:
Peace be on You, O Prophet, and also the Mercy of Allāh and His blessings. Blessings and peace on You, O Prophet of Allāh. Blessings and peace be on You, O beloved of Allāh. Peace and blessings be on You, O the best of Allāh's creations.

q	ق	*	z	ز		'	أء	*
k	ك		s	س		b	ب	
l	ل		sh	ش		t	ت	
m	م		ṣ	ص	*	th	ث	*
n	ن		ḍ	ض	*	j	ج	
h	ه		ṭ	ط	*	ḥ	ح	*
w	و		ẓ	ظ	*	kh	خ	*
y	ي		'	ع	*	d	د	
			gh	غ	*	dh	ذ	*
			f	ف		r	ر	

SHORT VOWELS	LONG VOWELS	DIPHTHONGS
a \ ـَ	a \ ـَا	aw \ ـَوْ
u \ ـُ	u \ ـُو	ai \ ـَيْ
i \ ـِ	i \ ـِي	
Such as: *kataba* كَتَبَ	Such as: *Kitab* كِتَاب	Such as: *Lawḥ* لَوْح
Such as: *Qul* قُلْ	Such as: *Mamnun* مَمْنُون	Such as: *'Ain* عَيْن
Such as: *Ni'mah* نِعْمَة	Such as: *Dīn* دِين	

* Special attention should be given to the symbols marked with stars for they have no equivalent in the English sounds .

Rasūlullāh, *Salla Allahu 'alaihi wa Sallam* (صَلَّى ٱللَّهُ عَلَيْهِ وَسَلَّم), and the Qur'ān teach us to glorify Allah ﷻ when we mention His Name and to invoke His Blessings when we mention the names of His Angels, Messengers, the *Saḥābah* and the Pious Ancestors.

When we mention the Name of Allah we must say: *Subḥāna-hū Wa-Ta'ālā* (سُبْحَانَهُ وَتَعَالَى), Glorified is He and High. In this book we write an ﷻ to remind us to Glorify Allah.

When we mention the name of Rasūlullāh ﷺ we must say: *Salla Allāhu 'alai-hi wa-Sallam,* (صَلَّى ٱللَّهُ عَلَيْهِ وَسَلَّم), May Allah's Blessings and Peace be upon him. We write an ﷺ to remind us to invoke Allah's Blessings on Rasūlullāh.

When we mention the name of an angel or a prophet we must say: *Alai-hi-(a)s-Salām* (عَلَيْهِ ٱلسَّلاَم), Upon him be peace. We write an ؑ to remind us to invoke Allah's Peace upon him.

When we hear the name of the *Saḥābah* we must say:
For more than two, *Raḍiya-(A)llāhu Ta'ālā 'an-hum,* (رَضِيَ ٱللَّهُ تَعَالَى عَنْهُمْ), May Allah be pleased with them.
For two of them, *Raḍiya-(A)llāhu Ta'ālā 'an-humā* (رَضِيَ ٱللَّهُ تَعَالَى عَنْهُمَا), May Allah be pleased with both of them.
For a *Saḥābī*, *Raḍiya-(A)llāhu Ta'ālā 'an-hu* (رَضِيَ ٱللَّهُ تَعَالَى عَنْهُ), May Allah be pleased with him.
For a *Saḥābiyyah*, *Raḍiya-(A)llāhu Ta'ālā 'an-hā* (رَضِيَ ٱللَّهُ تَعَالَى عَنْهَا), May Allah be pleased with her.
We write an ؓ to remind us to invoke Allah's Pleasure with a *Saḥābī*, a *Sahabiyah* or with *Saḥābah*.

When we hear the name of the Pious Ancestor (*As-Salaf as-Ṣāliḥ*) we must say.
For a man, *Raḥmatu-(A)llāh 'alai-hi* (رَحْمَةُ ٱللَّهِ عَلَيْهِ), May Allah's Mercy be upon him.
For a woman, *Raḥmatu-(A)llāh 'alai-hā* (رَحْمَةُ ٱللَّهِ عَلَيْهَا), May Allah's Mercy be with her.

Vocabulary

abstain (v) to do without, to decline, to refuse.

'Adāb: (n) good manners, decency, decorum.

'Ahl al-Bait: (n) The family of the Prophet ﷺ.

'Ālim: (n) an Islamic scholar.

'Aṣr: (n) the afternoon prayer: the time

authority (n) expert, specialist, master; rule, control, government; strength, influence.

'Āyah: (n) a verse of the Qur'ān

'Ayyām Tashriq: (n) The 11th, 12th, and 13th of Ẓhu al-Ḥijjah. Part of *'Īd al-Aḍḥa*, the animals are slaughtered and eaten and fasting is prohibited.

Bait Allāh: (n) the House of Allāh ﷻ; the Ka'bah

Bait al-Māl: (n) the Islamic treasury (Lit: the House of Wealth)

Bait al-Maqdas: (n) Jerusalem; the first *Qiblah* (Lit: the Sacred House).

balanced diet: (n) a program of eating that draws from each of the food groups

bondage: (n) slavery, confinement.

concept: (n) idea, notion, philosophy or theory.

cultivation: (n) planting, sowing; farming.

deprive: (v) to rob, seize, deny; refuse or withhold.

devote: (v) to apply, commit, dedicate.

Dhabiḥah: (n) slaughter in the Islāmic way.

Dhikr: (n) remembrance of Allāh ﷻ.

Dhu al-Ḥijjah: (n) The Twelfth month of the Islamic Calendar. The month of the *Ḥajj*.

Du'ā' (pl: 'Ad'iyah): (n) a personal prayer, calling upon God.

energy: (n) strength, power, potency.

enrage: (v) to anger, inflame, infuriate.

enjoin: (v) to command; to urge.

Fajr: (n) the dawn, the dawn prayer

Faqih (pl: Fuqahā'): (n) a scholar of *Fiqh*, a jurist

Farḍ: (n) something that is obligatory, such as fasting during *Ramaḍān* or the five daily prayers

Fiqh: (n) Islamic jurisprudence

full measure: (n) giving the fair amount in business transactions

genuine: (a) authentic, real.

Ḥajj: (n) the pilgrimage to Makkah; one of the five pillars of Islām.

Ḥājj: (n) a pilgrim.

Ḥalāl: (a) Lawful in Islām.

Ḥadith (pl:'Aḥādith): (n) The sayings (traditions) of the Prophet Muḥammad ﷺ

Ḥafiz: (n) One who has memorized the entire Qur'ān.
Al-Ḥajr al-'Aswad: (n) The Black Stone. It is located in the Ka'bah.
Ḥalq: (n) The cutting of the hair.
Ḥarām: (a) Unlawful in Islām.
heritage (n) ancestry, background; culture; history; lineage.
Hijrah: (n) The migration of the Prophet ﷺ and the *Ṣaḥabah* ﷺ from Makkah to Madīnah. The beginning of the Muslim calendar.
Ḥikam (n) Wisdom.
Ḥujjaj (n) plural of *Ḥājj* (pilgrims).

'Ibādāt: (n) acts of worship.
'Id: (n) Feast, celebration.
'Id al-'Aḍḥa: (n) Feast of the Sacrifice.
'Id al-Fiṭr: (n) Feast of the fast-breaking. This feast marks the end of *Ramaḍān.*
'Ifrād: (n) literally: Single. *Ḥajj* done without performing *'Umrah.*
'Ifṭār: (n) the breaking of the fast.
'Iḥrām: (n) two pieces of white sheets worn during the *Ḥajj.*
'Ijmā ' (n) consensus. That which all Muslim scholars can agree upon.
'Ijtihāh: (n) to exercise personal judgment based on the Qur'ān and *Sunnah.*
intelligence: (n) wisdom, mental capacity; reason.
intoxicants: (n) anything which causes loss of reason; anything which causes drunkenness.
'Imām: (n) leader of prayer; leader of the community; a great *Faqīh.*
incline: (n) angle. (v) to lean toward.
invalidation: (n) cancellation, reversal, negation.
'Ishā': (n) the night prayer.

Jamrāt: (n) the stone pillars at 'Aqaba which represent the *Shayāṭīn* (the Satans).
Jihād: (v): to struggle, to strive. Struggle in the Way of Allāh ﷻ.
Jihād an-Nafs: (n) the personal struggle within oneself to better oneself.

Lailat al-Qadr: The Night of Power. Special blessings are bestowed on the prayerful during this night of *Ramaḍān.* Its blessings are better than a thousand months.

Ka 'bah: (n) cube-shaped building located in the center of the *Masjid al-Ḥarām.* The point towards which all Muslims pray *(Qiblah).*
Khatib: (n) one who gives *Khutbah*, the sermons.
Khulafa': (n) Title of Muslim rulers. Allāh ﷻ viceregent.
Khutbah al-Wada': (n)The sermon of farewell, given by Rasūlullāh ﷺ during his last *Ḥajj.*
Kufr: (n) refusal to follow or disbelief in Allāh's commands.

Al-Madinah al-Munawwarah: literally, The Illuminated City, the name of the city of the Prophet ﷺ.
Maḥram: (n) a man whom a woman cannot marry due to nearness of relationship (i.e. brother, father, uncle, etc.)
Maqām Ibrāhim: (n) The place where Ibrāhīm's footprints are preserved near the *Ka'bah.*
Al-Masjid al-Ḥarām: (n) The Holy Mosque; the *Ka'bah* is located within it.

Masjid: (n) mosque.

Masjid al-' Aqṣā: (n) The site of the *Mi'rāj* (night journey/ascension) of Rasūlullāh ﷺ in Quds.

Masjid al-Qiblatain: (n) The *masjid* in which the order came to change the direction of the *Qiblah* from *Al-Quds* (Jerusalem) to the *Ka'bah* in Makkah.

Masjid Quba: (n) The first *masjid* built by Rasūlullāh ﷺ just outside Madīnah.

Masjid an-Nabi: (n) The first mosque built by Rasūlullāh ﷺ in Madīnah; he is buried in this mosque.

Mawlāna: (n) Our master, our leader, guide, protector.

menstruation: (n) a woman's monthly uterine discharge.

Mufassir: (n) one who can interpret the Qur'ān.

Mufti: (n) an Islamic scholar, capable of giving legal decisions on religious matters.

Multazim: (n) the area between the *Ka'bah* and the black stone wherein it is recommended that *Du'ā'* be made during *Ḥajj* or *'Umrah*.

Muqri (Qari): (n) a reader or reciter of the Qur'ān.

Mujtahid: (n) an Islamic scholar versed in the discipline of *'Ijtihād* (interpretation).

Muḥaddith: (n) an Islamic scholar versed in the science of *Ḥadīth* (of Islamic law).

Muttaqi: (n) one who has *Taqwā,* fear and consciusness for Allāh ﷻ. A righteous person.

Nafl: (a) voluntary.

Nisāb: (n) one's wealth that is considered taxable for payment as *Zakāh.*

Niyyah: (n) intention.

offspring: (n) children; family.

oppress: (v) to persecute, repress.

ordain: (v) to appoint, to command.

People of the Book: The Jews, Christians, and Sabeans.

perform: (v) to accomplish, to effect, to finish.

Pilgrimage: (n) to voyage, to journey to a place of spiritual significance.

possess: (v) to own.

posterity: (n) descendants, family, offspring.

precise: (a) exact, definite.

prescribe: (v) ordain.

preserve: (v) conserve, maintain, spare.

property: (n) belongings; anything owned.

provisions: (n) equipment, supplies.

purify: (v) to cleanse, to purge.

Qaḍā': (n) Making up for a missed worship such as *Ṣalāh* or *Ṣawm.*

Qāḍi: (n) a Judge.

Qarḍ Ḥasanah: (n) literally: A beautiful loan; a loan paid without interest.

Qirān: (a) one way of performing *Ḥajj.*

Qiyās: (n) Analogy. Reaching judgment using the Qur'ān and *Sunnah,* comparing it tc what might have happened had it occurred in the time of the Prophet ﷺ.

quenched (a) satisfied; thirst satisfied.

Rak'āh (pl: *Raka'āšt*) (n) A unit of the Prayer *(Salāh)* which involves a series of standing, bowing,

	two prostrations and sitting.
Ramaḍān:	(n) The ninth month of the Islamic calendar. The holy month of fasting.
recommend:	(v) to advise, to suggest, to urge.
repent:	(v) to regret, to lament, to rue.
require:	(v) to need; to command, to compel.
righteousness:	(n) a state of being moral, devout, pious and virtuous *Taqwā*.
ritual:	(n) ceremony, formality.
Rukn:	(n) A pillar of Islām. There are five: *Tashahhud, Ṣalāh, Ṣawm, Zakāh,* and *Ḥajj.*
Sab'ah Masājid:	(n) the Seven Mosques.
sacrifice:	(n) offering; (v) to give up, to renounce.
Ṣadaqah:	(n) something given away in charity for the pleasure of Allāh ﷻ
Ṣadaqah al-Fitr:	(n) that *Ṣadaqah* which is given before praying the *'Īd-al-Fitr* prayer.
Ṣaḥabah (singular Ṣaḥābi):	(n) the companions of the Prophet ﷺ.
S'ai:	(n) running between the hills of *Safa* and *Marwa* during *'Umrah* and *Ḥajj.*
Ṣalāh:	(n) prayer.
Salām:	(n) blessing and salutations, literally "peace".
sane:	(a) normal, rational. (Opposite of insane or crazy.)
Ṣawm:	(n) Fasting.
Shahid (pl: Shuhadā'):	(n) Martyr. Anyone who dies during struggle in the Way of Allāh ﷻ, a witneṣs.
Shaikh:	(n) A scholar of Islām, chief, head, elderly person.
Shaiṭān (pl: Shayātin):	(n) Satan, the Devil.
share:	(n) allotment, portion (v) to divide, to distribute equally.
Shawwāl:	(n) the Tenth month of the Islamic calendar, the first of *Shawwāl* is the day of *'Id.*
Shari'ah:	(n) Islamic law revealed by in the Qur'ān and detailed in the *Sunnah.*
Shirk:	(n) Polytheism. Associating other gods with the One God.
Ṣiyām:	(n) Fasting.
As-Ṣubḥ as-Ṣādiq:	(n) Pre-dawn; time to start the fast.
submit:	(v) to surrender, to obey, to yield to.
Suḥūr:	(n) the meal eaten before dawn by Muslims who fast the month of *Ramaḍān.*
Sunnah:	(n) traditions, sayings, and practices of the Prophet ﷺ..
Tamattu':	(n) literally: the interrupted *Ḥajj.* It consists of *'Umrah* then *Ḥajj,* but the pilgrim takes off the *Iḥrām* between the two.
Taqsir:	(n) the shortening (of the hair during *Ḥajj*).
Taqwā:	(n) God-consciousness; fear of Allāh ﷻ that encourages positive living.
Tarāwiḥ:	(n) voluntary prayers done following the *'Isha* prayer in Ramaḍān.
Ṭawāf:	(n) the circling of the *Ka'bah* seven times, as an act of worship in *Ka'bah.*
Thawāb:	(n) the reward for a good deed.
'Ummah:	(n) the Muslim community, the community in general.
'Umrah:	(n) a pilgrimage to Makkah in a period other than the one allotted for *Ḥajj.*
uncultivable:	(a) barren, dry, incapable of producing life.
'Ustādh:	(n) professor, teacher, scholar.
'Ūsul:	(n) sources, principle.
usury:	(n) money-lending made profitable by interest paid to the lender.

violate (v) to disobey, to defile, to sin against; to contaminate, to profane.

Waḥi: (n) Revelation. Inspiration given to the prophets by Allāh ﷻ.

Wājib: (n) an obligation; something that must be done.

Zakāh: (n) the mandatory giving of alms or charity to the poor. One of the Five Pillars of Islām.

Zamam: (n) the spring (now a well) which sustained Ḥājar ﷺ and her son Ismāīl ﷺ, when she was left in the barren desert in Makkah.

Ziyārah: (n) a holy visit. Here, it is the visit to Madīnah to honor the Prophet ﷺ.

Ẓuhr: (n) the noon prayer which consists of four *rak'āt, Farḍ* with two *Sunnah.*

INTRODUCING THE AUTHOR

Abidullah Ghazi, M.A. (Alig), M. Sc. Econ. (LSE London), Ph.D. (Harvard)
Tasneema K. Ghazi, M.A. (Alig), M. Ed. (Allahabad), Acd. Dip. (London), CAGS (Harvard), Ph.D. (Minnesota)

Dr. Abidullah Ghazi, Executive Director of IQRA′ International, and his wife, Dr. Tasneema Ghazi, Director of Curriculum, are co-founders of IQRA′ International Educational Foundation (a non-profit Islamic educational trust) and Chief Editors of its educational program. They have combined their talents and expertise and dedicated their lives to produce a Comprehensive Program of Islamic Studies for our children and youth and to develop IQRA′ into a major center of research and development for Islamic Studies, specializing in Islamic education.

Dr. Abidullah Ghazi, a specialist in Islamic Studies and Comparative Religion, belongs to a prominent family of the Ulama′ of India. His family has been active in the field of Islamic education, da ′wah, and struggle for freedom. Dr. Ghazi′s early education was carried in traditional Madaris. He has studied at Muslim University, Aligarh, The London School of Economics, and Harvard University. He has taught at the Universities of Jamia Millia Islamia, Delhi, London, Harvard, San Diego, Minnesota, Northwestern, Governors State and King Abdul Aziz University, Jeddah. He is a consultant for the development of the program of Islamic Studies in various schools anduniversities. He is a well-known community worker, speaker, writer and poet.

Mrs. Ghazi is a specialist in Child Development and Reading (Curriculum and Instruction). She has studied at the Universities of Aligarh, Allahabad, London, Harvard, San Diego, and Minnesota. She has taught in India, England, Jeddah, and the United States at various levels: kindergarten, elementary, junior, senior and university. Since her arrival in the USA in 1968, she has been involved with the schools of Islamic Studies providing them valuable advice and guidance. Working with children is her main interest.

Dr. and Mrs. Ghazi have a life-long commitment to write, develop and produce Islamic educational material and quality textbooks at various levels. Mrs. Ghazi has completed Pre-school, Kindergarten, and Elementary level Curricula and plans to produce an integrated curriculum for Junior and High School levels by 1998, Insha Allah. They have five children, Bushra, Rashid, Saba′ and twins, Suhaib and Usama. Their children provided them with their first experimental lab. They are also their co-workers.